HANDBOOK OF DECORATIVE DESIGN AND ORNAMENT

Handbook of
DECORATIVE DESIGN AND ORNAMENT

By Mary Jean Alexander

TUDOR PUBLISHING COMPANY
New York, N. Y.

Dedicated to a helpful and cooperative team —
Ruth, Bernie and George

Library of Congress Catalog Card Number 65-20752
ISBN: 8148-0395-4

Manufactured in the United States by Ganis and Harris, New York

Contents

CHAPTER ONE

Some General Aspects of Design

Design, in its broadest artistic sense, and decorative design, with which this book is concerned, are not the same. Design means the creation of a plan for the making of any object that is intended to have aesthetic merit and, if necessary, function properly. Two aspects are involved: the utilitarian and the decorative. Design may be structural and often implies three-dimensional form.

Decorative design, on the other hand, is not a thing in itself—it decorates something else. It requires space and a choice of line, form (used two-dimensionally), and sometimes color or value, arranged in a pleasing and orderly manner. It enhances, but does not originate. The field of decorative design embraces the basic devices, motifs and ideas from which all ornament and decoration are derived.

Decoration and ornament should be used only when they add to the appearance of whatever they are intended to decorate. The word decorative comes from the Latin word *decoratus*, which is close to the root of the word decorum; good decoration, well used, will also be decorous—fitting, becoming. Rightly used, the conformation of any decorative design or ornament will be suitable to the shape or structure of the object it decorates. It should

strengthen and emphasize the original design idea and never compete with it.

Decorative design seems to have been part of the earliest records of civilization and all evidence indicates that it goes far back into prehistoric times. While often treated as one, prehistoric and primitive design are not always the same. Prehistoric means simply the period before recorded history, and in the Western world covers the Stone Age and the

Unsuitable ornament destroys the beauty of a well-designed form

Metal Age. The Metal Age, sub-divided into the Early and Later Bronze Ages and the Early and Later Iron Ages, probably started in Europe around 1500 B.C. when the use of bronze was introduced. The Later Iron Age dates from 400 B.C. to 100 B.C. Primitive refers to the beginning and early stages of a civilization. In parts of the world today, there are groups of people who are in an early stage of development and their ornament is contemporary, but crude, simple and primitive in manner.

Some of the earliest designs evolved from practical operations. One of the most primitive and universally used of these is the pattern in squares resembling a checkerboard, called a check. It is probably the result of the pattern made by weaving rushes into mats—that is, by the crossing of one equal strip by another, at right angles. The pattern made by this arrangement can be easily reproduced as a surface effect, with a definite check appearing when color or value is added. It can be used in many ways, on almost any kind of material, and is

Primitive design is varied

Prehistoric design is often elegant

one of the few patterns that looks equally well flat—for example, on the floor, or vertical—on the wall.

Plaiting, netting, wattle and wicker ware and thonging are other functional processes that became designs. In the Bronze Age, lines were applied onto metal axe-heads that imitated the thongs that had been used in the Stone Age to bind the axe-head to the handle. The craftsmen who created these patterns were not responsible for their use as design. It was because the artists in the tribes found the structural lines both interesting and decorative and used them as ornament that they have become a permanent part of decorative design today.

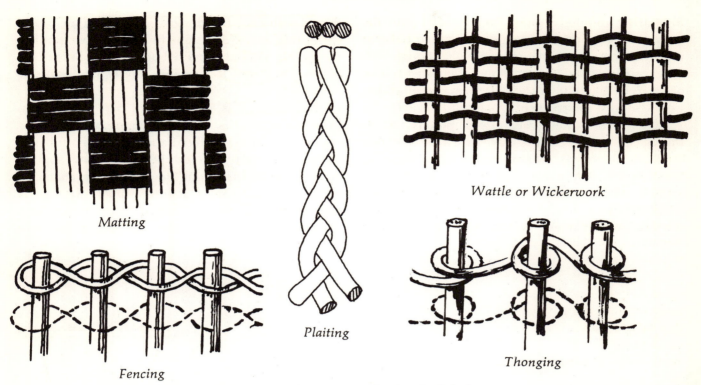

Matting

Wattle or Wickerwork

Fencing

Plaiting

Thonging

Some practical operations that inspired designs

Other early motifs that have come down to the present as design were created as a means of expressing ideas—that is, of presenting visually certain kinds of knowledge and mystical lore. Supernatural powers and the mysticism practiced by witch doctors came to be represented by many pictorial figures, both natural and stylized, and by geometric devices, such as the two crossed lines that became the cross. (Actually, primitive pattern work along geometric lines preceded the science of geometry.) All of these representational efforts contributed to the develop-ment of ornamental art, and many of them were used decoratively long after their significance was forgotten.

Vessels used for wine, water and oil, both in primitive and later civilizations, were ordinarily designed for function. To function properly a vessel was made with a hollow body, of a convenient size and shape for its purpose—pouring, dipping, carrying, etc.—and usually with a handle or handles strong enough for practical use. Some of these forms, particularly the Greek varieties, were highly

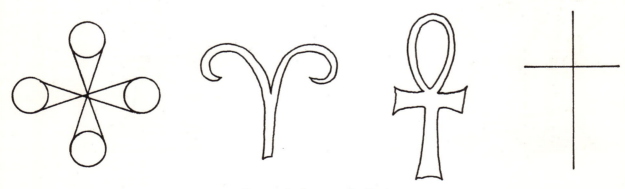

Early mystical or symbolic forms

decorative and have often found their way into ornament. The term *urn* is generally used today to refer to many kinds of such vessels, although they are classified under specific names. Drinking vessels, of entirely different but equally decorative shapes, were also used as ornament.

These vessels were generally of pottery. Many things can be done with clay, which is soft, that cannot be done with other materials. Each material possesses its own natural properties—hardness or softness, strength, density, resilience and texture. These qualities should determine, to some extent, the kind of ornament that is suitable, and often

should influence the design. The Egyptians made sculptured, stylized designs in their native granite; the Greeks worked roundly but precisely in marble; while Gothic and Renaissance motifs flowed in soft stone.

If a material is an important part of a design, in selecting motifs for its decoration only those appropriate to the material and which will enhance its natural beauty should be used. Any applied design should bring out the distinctive character of the material—have a definite rapport with it. A superficial relationship, instead of an honest and sincere one, will weaken the total design. Ruskin

A few vessel types used in design

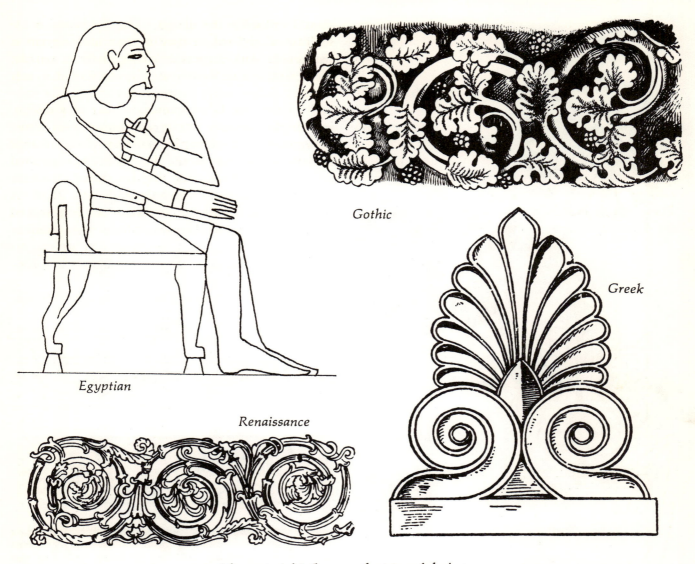

Gothic

Greek

Egyptian

Renaissance

The material influences the type of design

said bluntly, "If you don't want the qualities of a substance you use, you ought to use something else."

Modern technology, by the development of synthetics and processes that make possible an astounding degree of control in manufacture, has made materials much more flexible. But materials do react differently when design is being applied, and can't be treated in the same manner. Stone requires one kind of cutting stroke, wood another, and metal must be handled in still another way. The processes of manufacture also vary greatly. A good designer will not only be familiar with the qualities of his materials, but will also know about any manufactur-

ing processes that go into the finished product that he is designing or decorating.

Decorative design can be divided, in a general way, into two categories.

    1. *Decorative motifs*

    2. *Systems of arrangement,* or *patterns*

Pattern implies a design composed of one or more repeated devices arranged in orderly sequence. Such systems of arrangement may be limited or unlimited in area. Limited areas include borders or panels, or any space enclosed by a border. Unlimited areas include all-over or repeat patterns and stripes, any of which may be made of single units, groups of

Simple decorative motifs

units, or based on a continuous line.

The subject matter used in decorative design is unlimited. Any natural or artificial form, or one derived from a geometric arrangement of line, can be used, either singly or in combination. The only limitation is the lack of inventive capacity on the part of the designer. One can choose from a tremendous variety of forms—based on plants, fruits, animals, birds, insects, the human body; such artificial objects as trophies, ribbons, tassels, swords, shields; and dozens of geometric shapes. Furthermore, this vast number of forms can be combined in endless ways, making the possibilities truly infinite. The forms in this book are intended to suggest some of these design ideas and stimulate the imagination.

The aim of a designer is to create good design.

Bands and borders

All-over pattern

Good design, whether it be flat or three-dimensional, is achieved on the basis of principles and elements common to all art. The motifs and design devices included in this book, for example, are not necessarily good or bad in themselves. The way they are used in a design is what determines their merit and the success of the design, and to properly combine them it is necessary to refer to basic art principles and elements. Anyone who works with design, consequently, must know and thoroughly understand all of them, and be able to apply them correctly. They are: *unity, harmony, emphasis, subordi-*

Stripes

Enclosed space

nation and *dominance, contrast, variety, rhythm, balance, scale* and *proportion, line* and *form.* The importance of *value* in design will also be explained.

Unity.   Any good design, from the simplest to the most elaborate or intricate, has unity. This concept actually encompasses all other principles and elements of design. Mastering it will help in understanding and applying these other principles and elements, and conversely, the poor application of any of them will destroy a design's unity.

Unity is achieved by a choice and an arrangement of parts that produces a single, orderly whole. It has been called the cornerstone of design. It requires consistency of idea, line and form, and gives a feeling of oneness. Leonardo da Vinci defined it expressively as having a double function: "Every part is disposed to unite with the whole that it may thereby escape its own incompleteness." Each part must be essential in itself, and at the same time add to the total effect. A unified design will be a complete design.

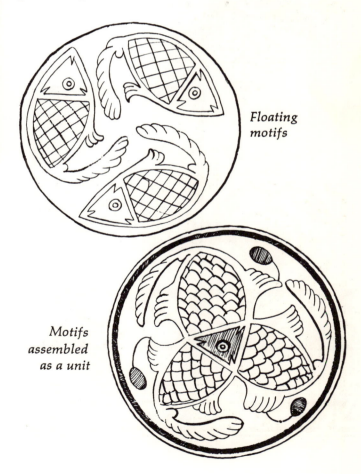

Floating motifs

Motifs assembled as a unit

The same forms can be inharmonious (above) or harmonious (right)

Motif overemphasized

Motif properly emphasized

Contrast in a border

There are several ways of effecting unity. The original plan must be logical and orderly. A definite center of interest that sets the character of the design will, if properly emphasized, help to assure a unified result. Repetition and similarity will often create unity, but too much of either can make a design uninteresting or monotonous.

Harmony. Harmony means the restful relationship of parts to one another and requires a balancing of straight, curved and diagonal lines when used together. It is essential to a unified design, but stops short of the oneness demanded by unity. The terms are not synonymous, although sometimes mistakenly used so. Harmony, just as unity, requires orderly arrangement and involves idea, line, form and, when used, value or color.

Emphasis—including *Dominance* and *Subordination.* Emphasis requires that one idea or design theme be dominant. Dominance is the effect of superior importance. The design should be planned so that the eye is irresistibly drawn to the basic theme, with the rest of the design seen in order of importance. Emphasis is imperative to unity. If all parts of a design, or even several parts, are of equal importance, there is a feeling of competition and the effect is confused and disturbing. The idea that dominates is given greater forcefulness through the right subordination of less important features. Subordination is the effect of inferior importance.

When working out a design, a good method is to start by evaluating the material to be used in order of importance, and decide at the beginning what will be the center of interest. Then determine how important each subordinate part will be. Each should give just the correct amount of emphasis to the central idea, so that all seem to take their rightful place in the composition as a whole.

Contrast. Important for emphasis, contrast is the quality of opposition of line and form, and when used, value or color. It is achieved by relating lines or forms of definitely different character and has the greatest effect when these lines or forms are placed next to each other. The further apart they are, the less the contrast. Value is also important to contrast. The purpose of contrast is to make one line, form, value or color stand out more sharply when used against another, giving more emphasis.

If a design has too much contrast, however, unity will be sacrificed.

Variety.   Variety is the lack of sameness—a combining of different ideas and qualities. It can be achieved through a choice of line, form, value and color, or through contrast. It is useful in furnishing vitality and sometimes excitement to a design. But it is like strong seasoning—the right amount, subtly used, will add interest; too much will ruin the finished product.

Variety in a design

Rhythm.   Rhythm is disciplined movement, with a recurrence of strong and weak elements—the measured repetition of accents. In any design, the arrangement of line and form forces the eye to follow from one point to another. Properly used, rhythm guides the eye so it sees the parts of the design in the best sequence. Rhythm results when all parts of a design are perfectly coordinated.

There are three general ways of achieving rhythm in design:

1.) through the repetition of line, form, pattern, value or color
2.) through progression of size or shape
3.) by means of a continuous basic line

Repetition is marked by a recurrence of patterns or accents, separated by spaces or different patterns. This is the simplest kind of rhythm, but unless it is used with imagination it may become monotonous. *Progressive* rhythm requires a gradual increase or decrease in the size or shape of a design. It is stronger than rhythm by repetition, allows for more originality, but is more difficult to use successfully. *Continuous line* rhythm is often made mainly of curves and usually gives a flowing effect. Frequently more than one kind of rhythm is used in a design. The human body has a natural rhythm, but much early art based its rhythms on animals or plants.

Balance.   Balance denotes the equilibrium of elements. In design it requires a harmonious arrangement of parts around a center or central axis, giving the appearance of equal distribution. Balance in any design is necessary to give it repose. Lack of balance gives a feeling of restlessness which makes the viewer uncomfortable, although he may not realize why. It is a quality that people react to instinctively. It is absolutely essential to unity.

There are two kinds of balance: symmetrical or

RHYTHM

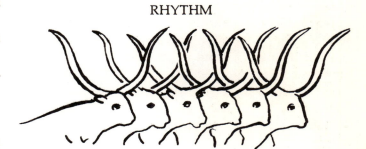

1. *Repetition*

2. *Progression*

3. *Continuous line*

Asymmetrical balance

Symmetrical balance

formal and asymmetrical or informal. Symmetrical balance requires the equal division of form, size and arrangement of parts, and implies identical halves —that is, forms of similar design and equal size on either side of a center line or focal point, and at an equal distance from it. Symmetrical balance is restrained and dignified and is often used where formality is desired. It can be static and inflexible, but many beautiful designs, from a tiny dressgoods pattern to the architecture of a room, are symmetrical.

Asymmetrical balance, also called optical or occult, creates a sense of equilibrium by the arrangement of two sets of forms of different size and shape (or value or color) on either side of an axis, so that they seem equal in importance. It is more casual, more imaginative and more difficult to use well than symmetrical balance. There are no real rules for arranging forms asymmetrically. The best way is to experiment until the two sides appear to have a good relationship to each other.

Scale and Proportion. Scale and proportion—relative qualities—are easiest to understand if taken together. Scale indicates a *size* relationship, proportion a *shape* relationship. Scale refers to the relationship, as to size, of each part of a design to the other parts and to the whole that contains it. Good scale requires that the sizes of all parts of a design be related in a satisfying way.

Proportion refers to the relationship of the shapes or areas within a design to each other and to the total unit. Good proportion has areas sufficiently alike to have something in common and still different enough to be interesting. The theory of

the Golden Mean or Golden Section, evolved by the designers of ancient Greece, is an accepted guide to good proportion. Two areas or lines used together are most effective if one is more than half and less than two thirds of the other; more exactly, if the smaller is to the larger as the larger is to the whole.

A simple method of determining the Golden Mean of a line with the aid of a right angle triangle and a compass is as follows: Draw two lines of equal length at right angles, marking the three points A, B and C. Extend line AB one half its length, establishing point D. With D as a center, and DC as a radius, draw arc CE. E bisects AB at its Golden Mean.

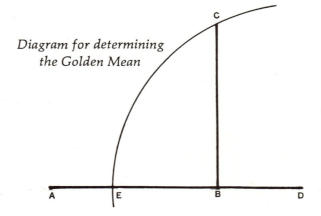

Diagram for determining the Golden Mean

Line and Form. Line and form, with color and value, provide the basic components of decorative design. Any design, whether flat or three-dimensional, requires space. Assuming adequate space, *line* supplies the simplest and most intrinsic element of design. It governs the shape of all flat design and is the basis for all decorative ornament. *Form* is the shape itself of an area or three-dimensional volume, as defined by the lines that surround it.

Lines are straight or curved. Straight lines may be vertical, horizontal or diagonal. They are stronger and more direct than curved lines. Vertical lines are structural, seem to be reaching upward and have the most strength. Horizontal lines are tranquil, less strong and more restful. Diagonal lines are lines of action and unless they are conclusively stopped usually keep the eye moving, giving a disturbing effect. They can readily become too important in a design, and when they do, destroy its unity.

Curved lines are made mathematically or freely, by hand. They are lighter and livelier than straight lines. Mathematical curves are made with an instrument, from any part of the arc of a circle or an ellipse. Freehand curves, as their name indicates, are freely drawn and may be commonplace or beautiful. Beautiful freehand curves are subtle and there is no end to their variety. Improperly used, curves may make a design restless. They can give a feeling of airiness, but they haven't the appearance of strength and too many may make a design seem weak rather than airy. Curves should always be planned carefully in relation to any straight lines that accompany them.

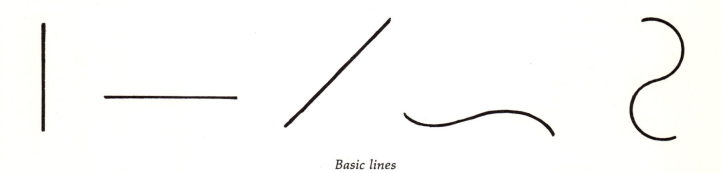

Basic lines

Form is the shape of an area or three-dimensional volume, as defined by the lines that give it a distinctive appearance. An object is recognized and identified by its form. Straight lines make such forms as triangles, squares, pentagons and various less common figures such as rhombi and trapezoids. Curved lines form circles, ellipses and ovals. Vertical forms are more dynamic than horizontal forms.

Scale and proportion: 1. badly scaled frame, 2. badly proportioned mat and badly scaled frame, 3. good scale and proportion relationships

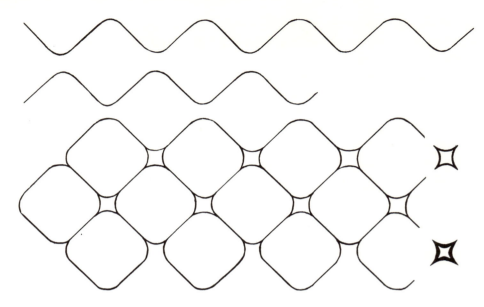

Curved and straight lines are often combined. The regular wavy line shown here *(above)* has strength in itself. Two of these lines facing each other appear to have less strength. But when the straight sides are connected by curved lines, not only does an interesting pattern result, but two additional forms can be isolated from it.

Value. When color is used, its value influences the total design effect. Value is the degree of lightness or darkness in a color, varying in this book from the lightest gray to black. The way in which value is used in a design is very important. Value can completely change the appearance of adjacent areas. It is important to unity. Carelessly used, it will make a design restless and completely destroy the unity. When contrast is needed, value can supply it.

Different use of value can completely change the appearance of a design

CHAPTER TWO

Basic Geometric Forms

HE IMPORTANCE of geometric forms in design is primary. Any pattern which consists of a repeated motif or group of motifs is based on geometric arrangement. (The many different kinds of such arrangement are discussed in Chapter Seven, which covers all-over and repeat designs.) But individual geometric forms and their possible combinations provide an incalculably vast reservoir of design devices themselves. The circle, triangle and square are almost universally recognized; other geometric forms are well-known, some better than others. For easy reference, those used in decorative design will be defined and illustrated, and in some cases their construction, and ways of dividing them, explained.

A *point* is too small to have recognizable shape. If it is made large enough to detect as a shape, it becomes a circle or appears to take some other form, and is no longer a point. In decorative design, a point refers only to location.

A *line* may be straight (vertical, horizontal or diagonal) or curved (mathematical or freehand).

Straight lines used continuously can become a fret or a zigzag design, with many possible variations. Straight lines with sharp angles, particularly of the zigzag kind, may give a feeling of nervous movement,

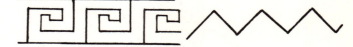

and if not used with care will disrupt the rhythm, harmony, unity, or all three, of a design. Used together, straight lines may be parallel, perpendicular, or at oblique angles to one another. Such lines often fool the eye. When a vertical line is placed next to a horizontal line of the same length, the vertical appears longer. When the vertical is directly above or below the horizontal, at its center, the apparent difference is exaggerated.

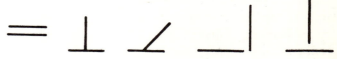

Curved lines, when continuous, may be wavy or ripply, twisted, braided, scalloped, spiral, U or S shaped. Softly curved lines are gentle and more feminine than sharper curves, which have a vigorous quality. The same curved lines swelling outward seem fuller than when they curve inward.

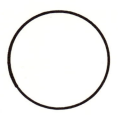

A *diameter* is any straight line passing from one side of the circle to the other through the center.

A *radius* is any straight line leading from the center to the circumference.

A *chord* is a straight line that intersects the circumference at any two points.

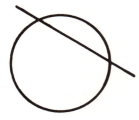

An *arc on chord* is the distance on the circumference bounded by a chord.

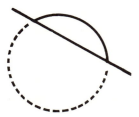

A *circle* is a plane figure bounded by a single curved line, every point of which is equidistant from the point at the center. Commonly called a circle, the line which makes the circle is the circumference. Except in construction, the word circle in this book will be used to refer to both the total area and the circumference. Parts of the circle are the diameter, radius, chord, arc on chord, segment and sector.

A *segment* is the plane area of the circle cut off by a chord.

A *sector* is the area bounded by two radii and a section of the circumference.

When a continuing straight or curved line meets the outside of the circumference at only one point, it is *tangent* to it. Two circles may be tangent to each other. Circles are *concentric* when they have the same center and different radii. They are *eccentric* when they partly coincide but have different centers.

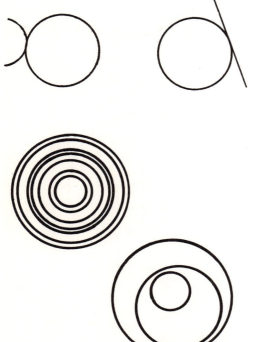

To find the center of a circle, draw two equal chords that intersect or meet on the circumference. Divide each into two equal parts, and draw perpendicular lines from each center point. The two lines intersect at the center of the circle.

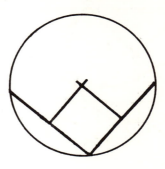

Any part of the arc of a circle can be used in design. To divide a given length of an arc into two equal parts, describe arcs from point A above and below the given arc. Do the same using point B as a center and the same radius. Connect the two points where these arcs intersect.

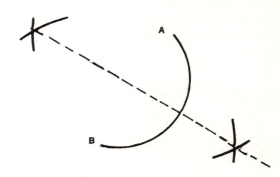

An *ellipse* is a plane form enclosed by a line with a radius of curvature that is continually changing. Since the ellipse requires more knowledge of geometry than some of the simpler forms, it appeared later in design.

There are several ways to construct an ellipse. One of the simplest *(diagram on p. 22)*: draw two adjacent squares. Connect the corners inside each with diagonals. Using A and B as centers and AC as a radius, draw arcs CD and EF. Using G as a center and GE as a radius, draw arc CE, and with

H as a center and the same radius, draw arc FD to complete the ellipse.

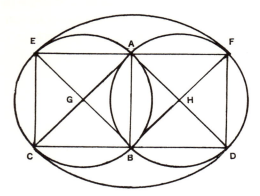

An *oval* is not the same as an ellipse, although the words are often used interchangeably. The root of the word oval is *ovum* (egg) and the oval is not symmetrical as is the ellipse, but eggshaped. To construct an oval draw a circle, the arc of which determines the larger end of the oval. Draw two chords, AC and BC. Using A as the center draw arc BE; using B as the center draw arc AD; and using C as the center draw arc DE that connects the previous two arcs, completing the oval. The radius of each arc is determined by the line with which it connects.

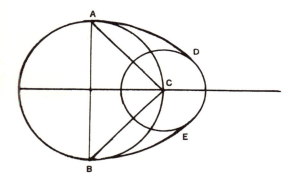

A *spiral* is the path of a point that winds or circles around an axis or center point while gradually and continuously receding from it. Spirals can be drawn geometrically with 2, 3, 4 or 5 centers, depending on how fast the curve should recede. With A as a center and AB as the radius, draw a half circle. With B as a center and BC the radius, continue the line with another half circle. Using A and B alternately as the center, continue making half circles, with radii that

connect with and continue each previous half circle, until the spiral is the size desired.

For spirals with more than two points, consult

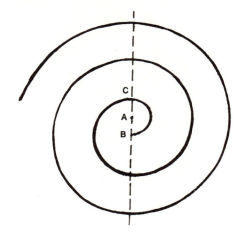

the diagrams and follow the same procedure as above.

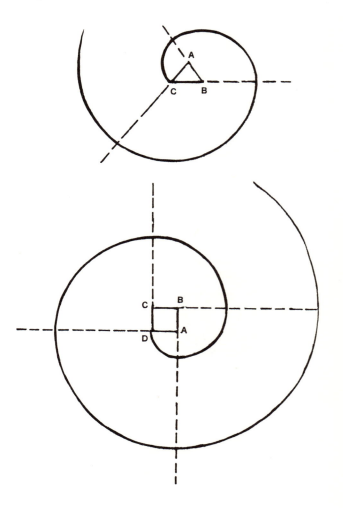

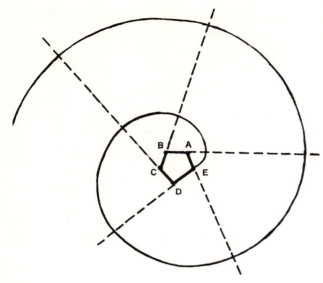

To bisect an angle, use O as a center and with any suitable radius draw an arc connecting the two sides of the angle. Using A and B as centers, and a radius greater than one-half AB, draw intersecting arcs to make point C. The line connecting C and O bisects the angle.

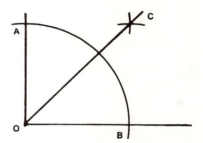

An *angle* is the figure or shape made by two straight lines coming together at a point. There are three basic kinds of angles.

1. A *right angle* has sides perpendicular to one another, and covers 90 degrees.

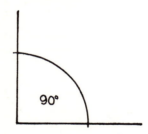

2. An *acute angle* is less than 90 degrees.

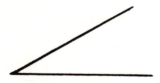

3. An *obtuse angle* is greater than 90 degrees.

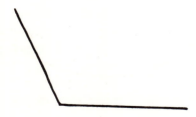

Triangles. The linear geometric form with the fewest sides and angles is the triangle. There are four kinds of triangles:

1. *Equilateral triangle,* with all sides and angles equal.

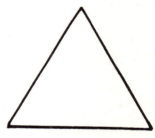

2. *Right angle triangle,* with one right angle, two equal acute angles and two equal sides.

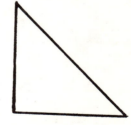

3. *Isosceles triangle,* with no right angle, but two equal sides and two equal angles.

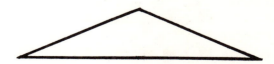

4. *Scalene triangle,* with no two sides or angles equal.

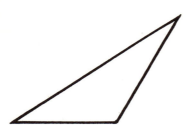

A *square* has four equal sides meeting in right angles. The square and the circle are the two most fundamental forms in decorative design, and with their variations, subdivisions and combinations are used more than any other forms. The square can be subdivided and arranged in countless ways. One large square divided into smaller squares, eleven on each side, can be arranged in more than 500 different ways, using only two colors, or simply black and white.

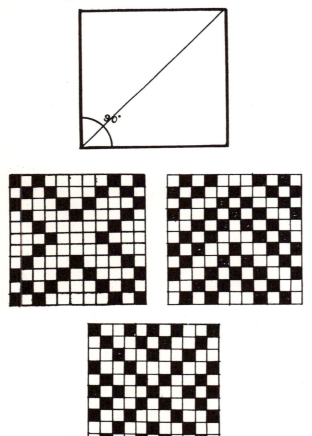

The term *polygon* covers all plane figures with more than four angles and sides.

A *pentagon* is a polygon with five sides and angles. To construct a pentagon, draw a circle with diameter AB and radius CD at right angles to it. Bisect CB, creating point E. Using E as a center and ED as a radius, draw an arc crossing AC at point F. With radius DF and D as a center, draw an arc crossing the circumference at G. With the same radius, step off points along the circumference from G to H, H to I, etc., which will divide it into five equal parts. Connect adjacent points to construct pentagon.

A five-pointed star can be made by drawing chords connecting every other point on the circumference.

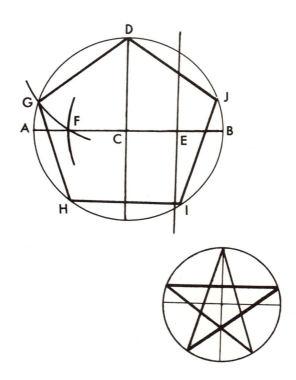

A *hexagon* is a polygon with six sides and angles. To construct a hexagon, draw a circle. Add vertical diameter AB, and step off radius AC along the circumference from A to D, D to E, etc. Connect adjacent points. Or, using the 60 degree side of a 30/60 triangle, draw lines DF and EG through center C and connect circumference points as before.

A six-pointed star can be made by connecting every second point on the circumference.

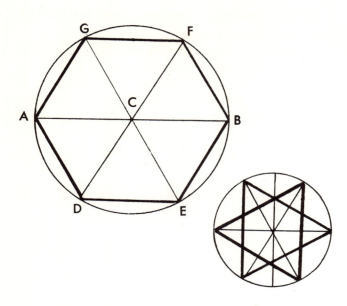

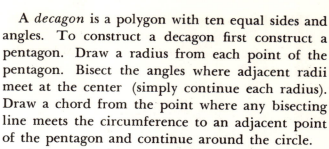

A *decagon* is a polygon with ten equal sides and angles. To construct a decagon first construct a pentagon. Draw a radius from each point of the pentagon. Bisect the angles where adjacent radii meet at the center (simply continue each radius). Draw a chord from the point where any bisecting line meets the circumference to an adjacent point of the pentagon and continue around the circle.

A ten-pointed star can be made by connecting every third point. A less common kind is made by connecting every second point.

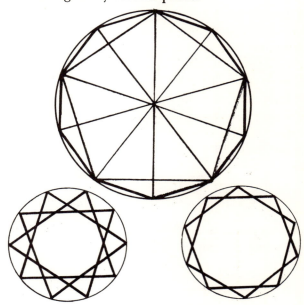

An *octagon* is a polygon with eight sides and angles. To construct an octagon draw a circle and add vertical and horizontal diameters AB and CD. Bisect each right angle at center E, letting each line intersect the circumference. Connect adjacent points along the circumference.

An eight-pointed star can be made by connecting every third point. A less common kind of eight-pointed star can be made by connecting every second point.

A *duodecagon* is a polygon with twelve equal sides and angles. To construct a duodecagon draw a circle with diameters AB and CD at right angles. With centers A, B, C and D, and the same radius as the circle, draw four arcs. Connect all consecutive points along the circumference.

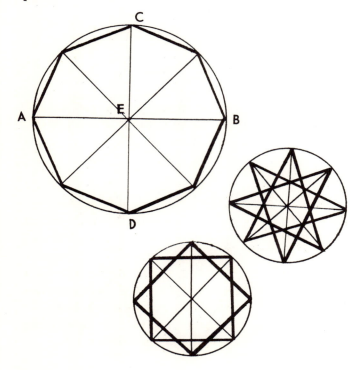

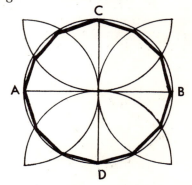

Some other geometric forms are frequently used in decorative design:

The *rhombus,* also called a diamond or lozenge, is probably the most common of these. A rhombus is a parallelogram with oblique angles and all sides equal.

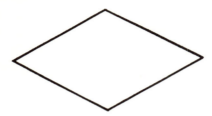

A *rhomboid* is a parallelogram with oblique angles and only opposite sides equal.

A *trapezoid* is a plane figure with four sides, two of which are parallel.

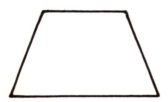

A *trapezium* is a plane figure with four sides, no two of which are parallel.

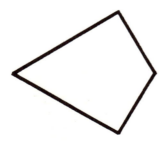

A *trefoil* is a form with three rounded petals.

A *quatrefoil* is a form with four rounded petals.

A *cinquefoil* is a form with five rounded petals.

An *arch* is a curved structure used as a support over an open space. Several kinds are commonly found in decorative ornament.

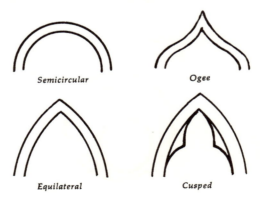

Semicircular   Ogee

Equilateral   Cusped

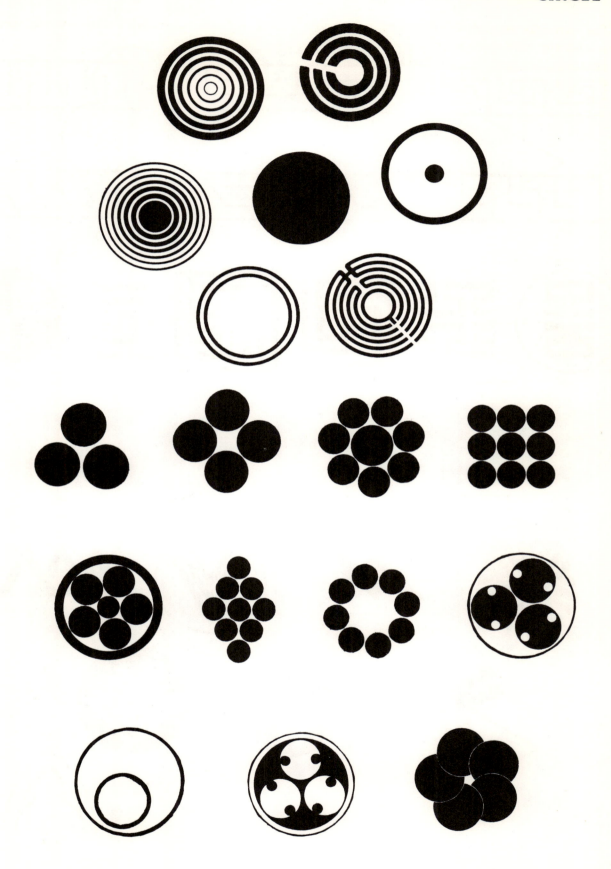

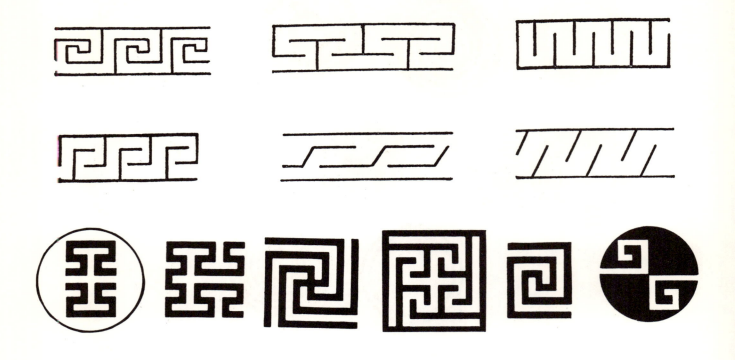

ZIGZAG AND CHEVRON

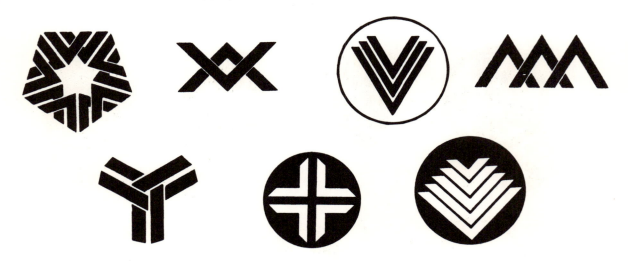

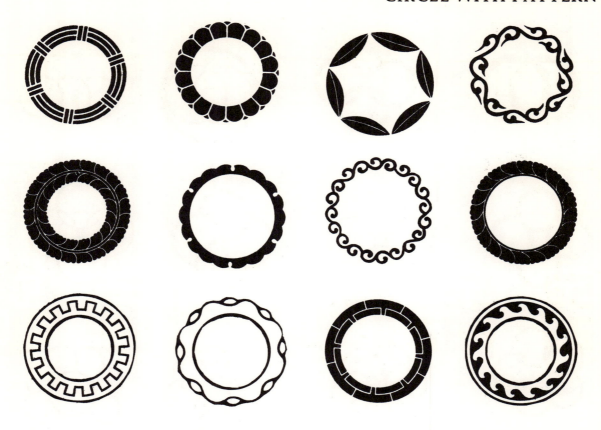

OVAL

CRESCENT

STAR

CHAPTER THREE

Forms Based on Nature

ALL THROUGH the ages man's natural environment has been a principal and vital source of design motifs. Although some primitive peoples ignored nature in favor of plain geometric arrangements, man, at every stage of civilization, seems generally to have been sufficiently impressed by the natural beauties that surrounded him to attempt to reproduce them in his ornament — sometimes crudely, sometimes with fine skill.

However, no sharp line can be drawn between natural and geometric forms because many forms combine both, and natural ones often become geometric in design. The basic distinction between the two lies in the fact that one is representational, the other is not. Geometric forms are not representational. Decorative design based on natural forms represents actual objects such as flowers, foliage, fruit, humans, animals and fish. The vast majority of these objects are organic, or living. But inorganic nature also provides beautiful models—softly rippling water, clothes hanging on a line, waves breaking on the shore, drifting sands and plowed fields, clouds or snowflakes, for example.

Natural forms are used in ornament in two dif-

ferent ways: realistically or literally, and conventionalized. Realistic forms copy nature as accurately as possible. Inorganic forms are generally used realistically. When a natural form is simplified or adapted to fit its use in a design, it is called conventionalized or stylized. There are degrees of stylizing. A slightly stylized motif will appear very much like a natural one, while one that is severely treated may be scarcely recognizable.

Natural forms are difficult to use realistically in design since it is not always possible to copy nature accurately and create a successful pattern. One noted 19th-century authority says that "the more perfect the imitation, the greater the mistake." Another says that only conventional representations of flowers or natural objects should be used and that whenever this has not been done, design has become decadent. The successful designer converts natural forms into appropriately ornamental or decorative ones.

In adapting some forms, particularly floral and foliage, for use in certain kinds of design, elaboration, rather than simplification, is used. Developing a design by this means requires care to prevent its becoming overdone and excessively ornate. Elaborate design has rarely been executed successfully, but there are some examples, notably from 18th-century Italy and France, that have beauty and charm. In combining flowers, fruits and foliage in elaborate designs, it is necessary to use them all with a feeling of consistency. Two methods of achieving this kind of elaboration are the turning over and curling up of the edges of all foliage, and the using of large, bold masses broken up by a smaller all-over pattern.

A good designer should be able to do his own conventionalizing, whether simple or elaborate. It is important to be familiar with historic design, but no matter how beautifully done, it is not necessary to copy it. Imagination and an original approach are essential to successful conventionalizing, which requires much more than the flattened detail of a natural form and an arbitrary arrangement of parts according to a diagram. The other extreme is to consider anything natural as being irregular. Where untidiness is found in nature, it is usually accidental and back of it is order and a unified design—which is what the designer should observe. Nature is basically orderly.

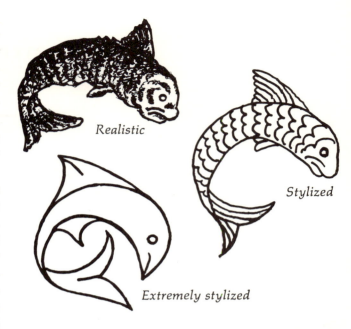

Realistic

Stylized

Extremely stylized

Elaboration (Silk Damask, 16th century)

Certain design principles can be seen in the forms of nature that are helpful in adapting them. That of radiation in growth is probably the most readily seen. The petals of a flower, leaves and some shells are examples. Lines may radiate from a single point, from a center line to both sides, or from an off-center line to one side.

The acanthus leaf is a classic example of ornament taken from nature. Introduced into design and beautifully stylized by the Greeks, it has since been used continuously in decorative art. As adapted, it sometimes bears little resemblance to the actual acanthus leaf, of which there are several different varieties. But the shapes and serrations of all of them lend

Radiation in nature

Beautiful natural forms also have well-proportioned distribution of areas, tangential curvature, and graceful lines—all good features to carry into a design.

Some natural forms can more readily be adapted for use as ornament than others. Certain flowers, such as the daisy, primrose or tulip, are unmistakably ornamental, with a definite character. Some plants and leaves are so well-defined that they seem conventionalized in their natural form. Such animals as the lion and the ram, and such fish as the dolphin or crab are easily applied to design. Other forms are less emphatic and lose all their character when used as ornament.

The forms illustrated in this book cover a multitude of types of growing things. Many kinds of foliage, such as leaves, vines, lichen and seaweed, as well as flowers, fruits and vegetables, provide a variety of forms suitable for ornament. Animals, birds and fish offer a vast assortment of design ideas. The human form, from a small cherub to a full figure, and many kinds of faces, some stylized as masks, are found in decorative design. Parts of the human body are also combined with animal forms, creating such figures as the centaur and the sphinx. The grace, movement and feeling of strength in these natural, living forms make them excellent models for ornament.

themselves equally well to design ranging from the well-known Corinthian capital to a tiny supporting detail.

Two acanthus leaves are shown here with several adaptations done at various times in different countries *(overleaf)*.

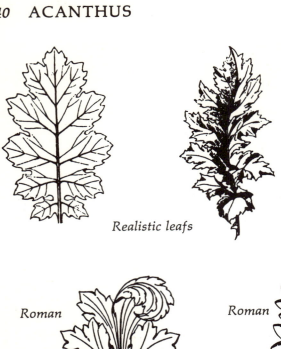

Realistic leafs

Naturalistically treated

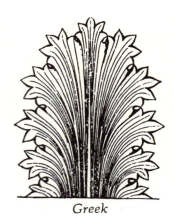

Greek

Roman

Roman

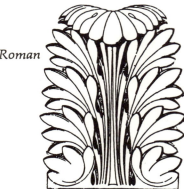

Roman

German Rococo

Gothic

Late French Renaissance

French Renaissance (Torus moulding)

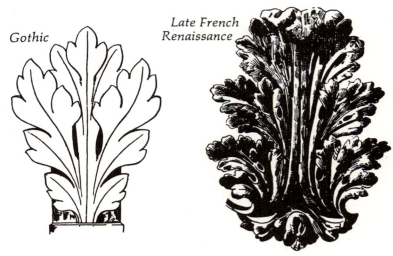

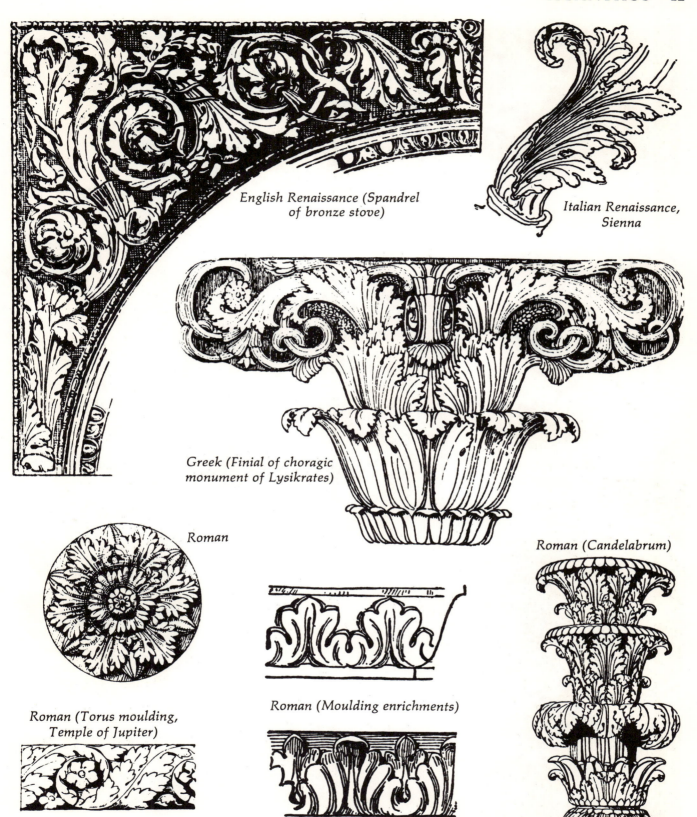

English Renaissance (Spandrel of bronze stove)

Italian Renaissance, Sienna

Greek (Finial of choragic monument of Lysikrates)

Roman

Roman (Candelabrum)

Roman (Torus moulding, Temple of Jupiter)

Roman (Moulding enrichments)

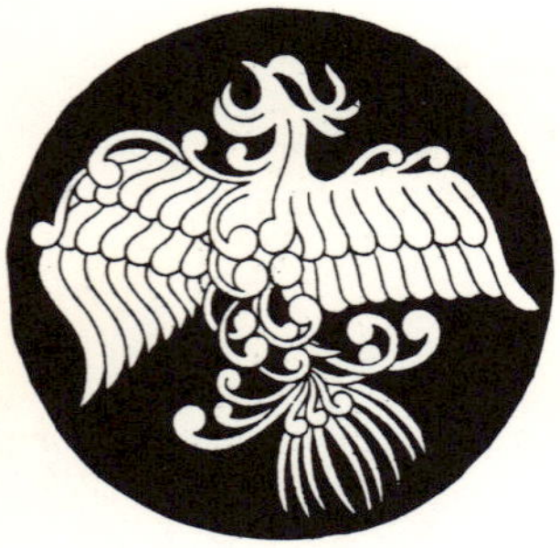
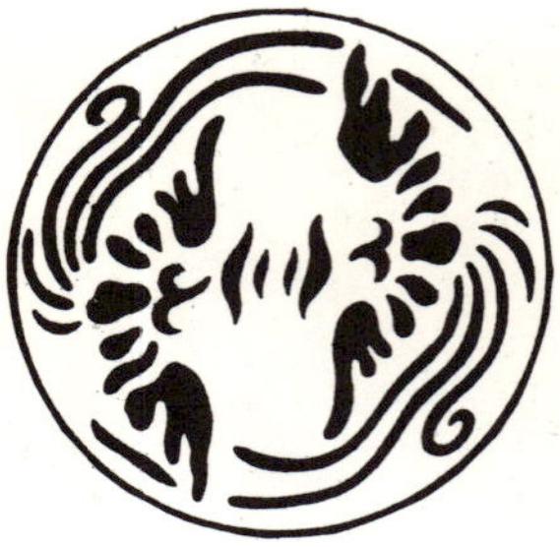
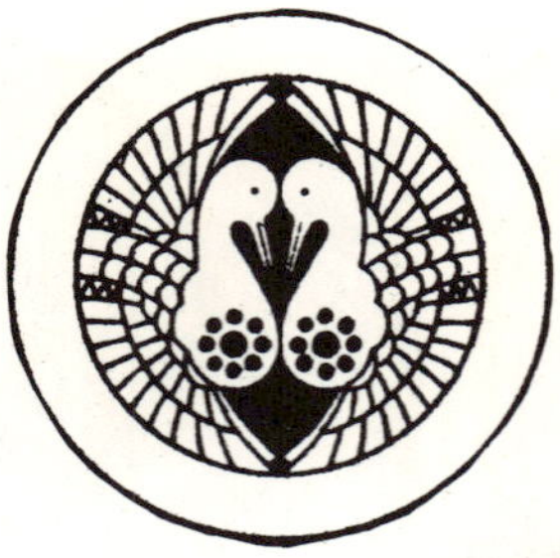
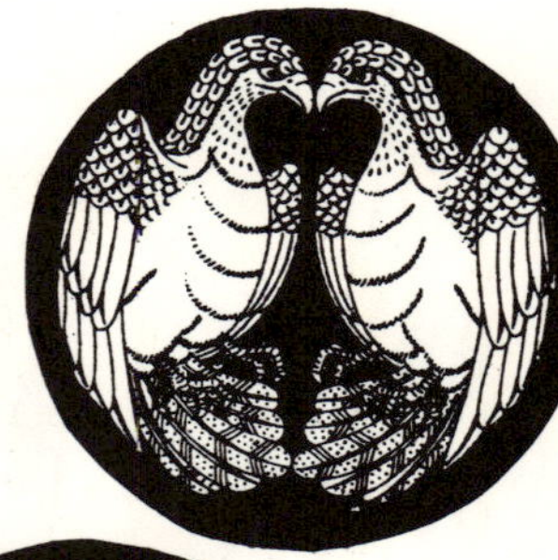
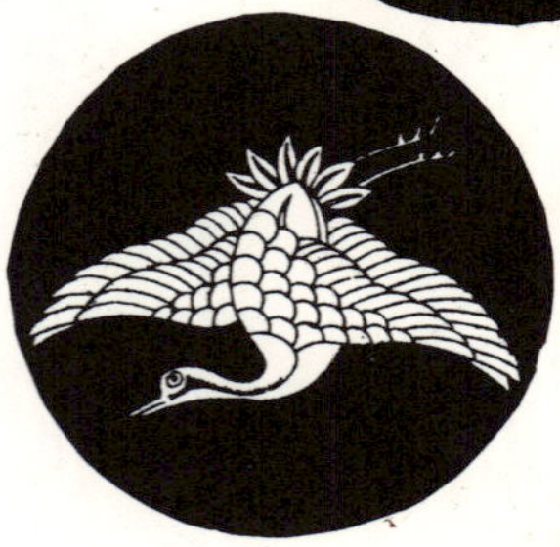
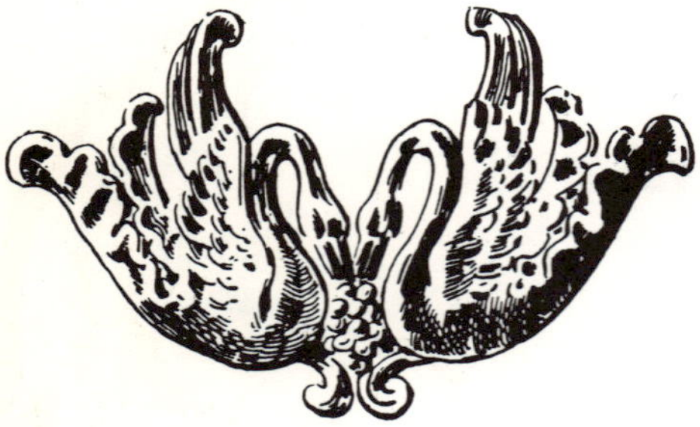
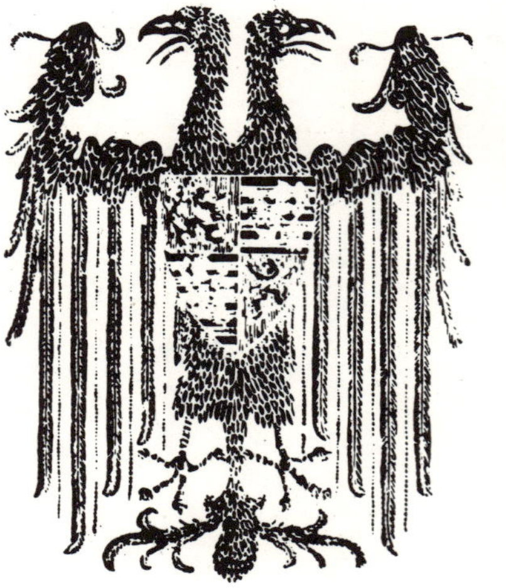
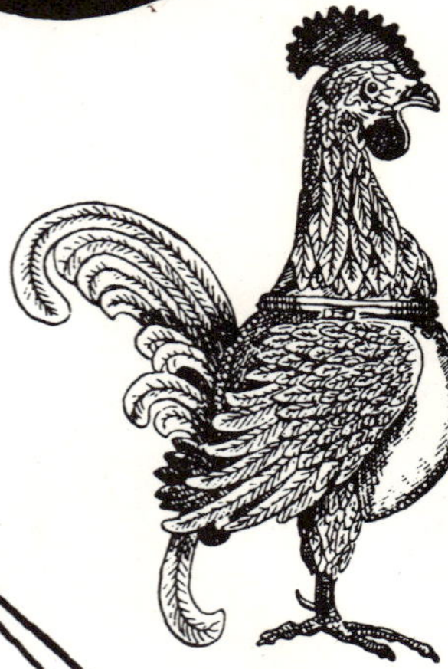
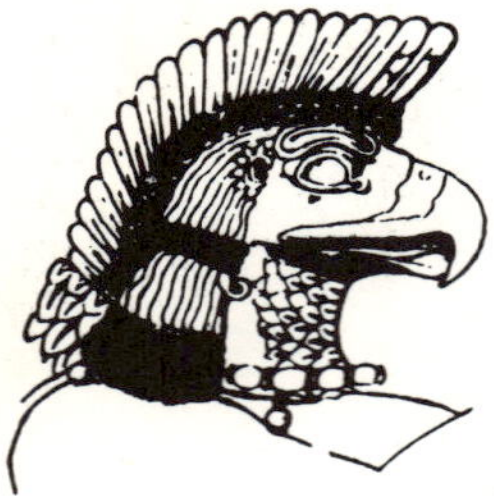
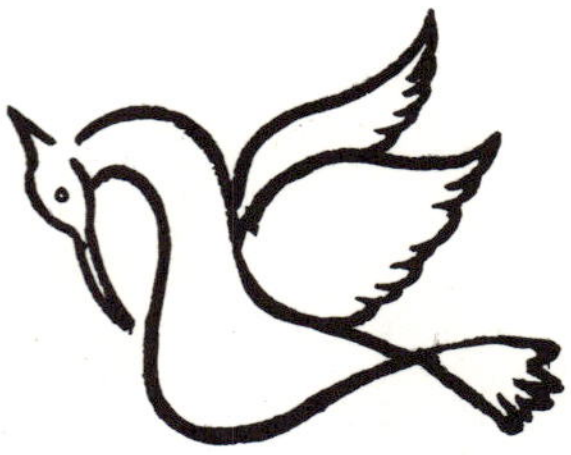
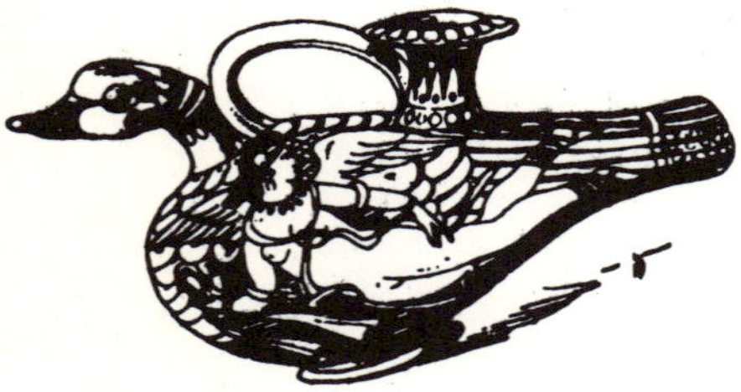
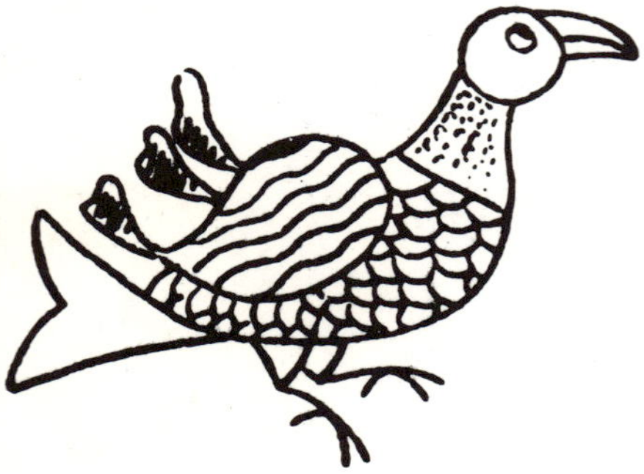
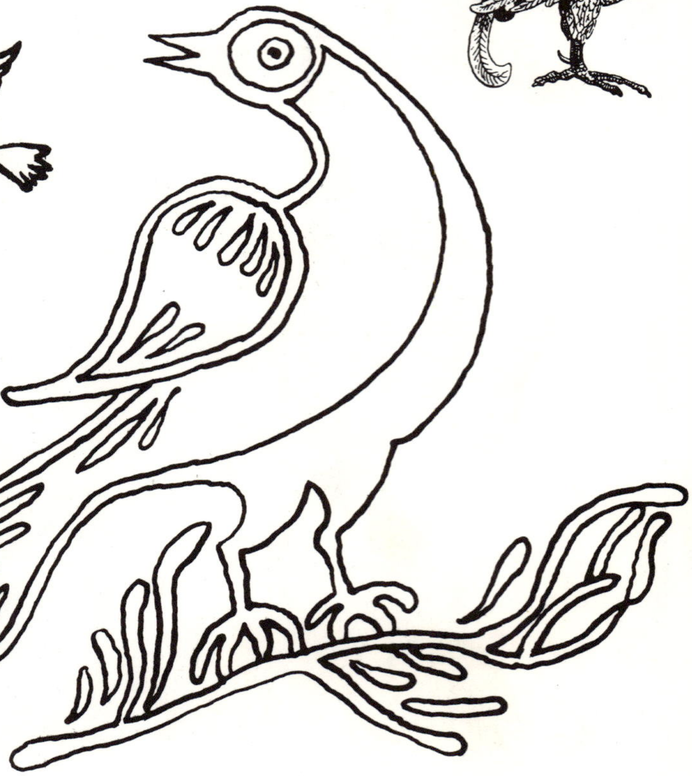

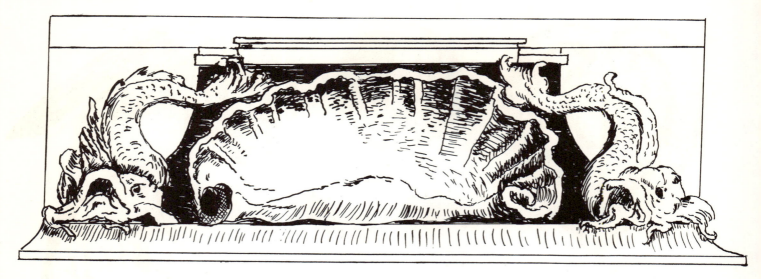

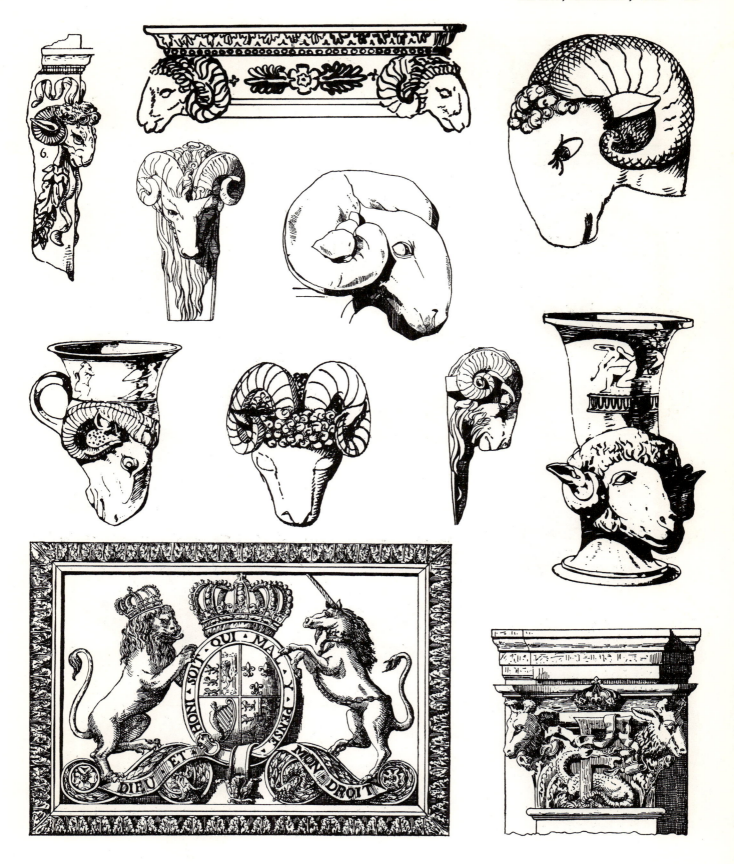

CHAPTER FOUR

Miscellaneous Forms

ERTAIN KINDS of ornamental forms are neither exclusively geometric nor based on natural forms. Many are derived from man-made objects, such as fans, bells, tassels, or musical instruments. Others are based on architectural elements, often those used either to support part of a design, such as a console, or to complete one, such as a finial.

Most such forms are already stylized in their original shapes and are decorative when used naturally. But many can be conventionalized further. When this is done, they tend to become geometric. The objects that these forms are based on are usually familiar and easily recognized.

Certain of the artificial objects included in this miscellaneous group were frequently used in trophies and symbols. A trophy was originally a memorial of a victory in war, and consisted of arms and other spoils taken from the enemy and hung on a nearby tree or pillar. Eventually, this custom led to the creation of ornamental panels of wood or stone, carved or painted, that depicted such weapons. Since these panels were often highly decorative they gradually came to be included in architectural design.

In the 18th century, trophy panels became purely decorative, with little war or memorial connotation. The designs contained the implements and tools of pastoral life or agriculture; or the symbols of love, the arts—music, drama, painting, sculpture, etc.—science, hunting or fishing. These trophy panels, often exquisitely carved, sometimes painted in delicate soft tones or gilded, were imaginative, beautifully designed and an important part of the ornament of the time.

A symbol is a material object that represents something immaterial or abstract. Although natural objects and geometric forms are most often used as symbols, a number of artificial objects are also used. The symbols for the pastoral or the agricultural life; for example, include the plow, the sickle and the scythe; the arts are represented by musical instruments, tragic and comic masks, brushes and palettes, and so on. Of the many religious symbols the most common is the cross, used in a wide variety of ways. The Medieval and Renaissance trade guilds had their own symbols, based either on the tools used or on the products made, or both. A great deal of imaginative creativity was used in the designing of both symbols and trophies.

Abstract ornament also falls into this category of miscellaneous forms. No examples have been included in this book, however, since the abstract designer creates his own devices independently of traditional motifs.

Below are several lists of man-made objects frequently used in design. Most of them are illustrated in the following pages.

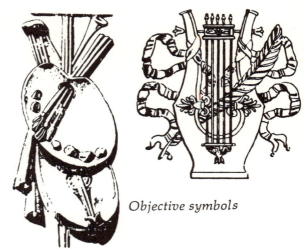

Objective symbols

WAR
helmet
bow and arrow
sword
dagger
scimitar
chariot
drum

ROMANCE
cupid's arrow
cupid's bow
ribbons
bows
tassels
fringes
garlands
festoons
swags
wreaths

ARTS AND TRADES
musical instruments
palette and brush
carpenter's tools
t-square
sickle
scythe
hoe
shovel

ARCHITECTURAL
anthemion
baluster
cartouche
console
finial
medallion
pediment
pilaster
base
shaft
capital
flutes
reeds
beads

MISCELLANEOUS
urn
tripod
scale
crown
bell
oar
kite
sailboat
cornucopia
scroll
fan
key
hat
parasol

Abstract symbols

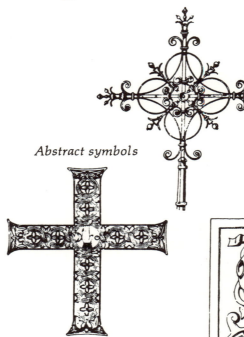

Trophy panels

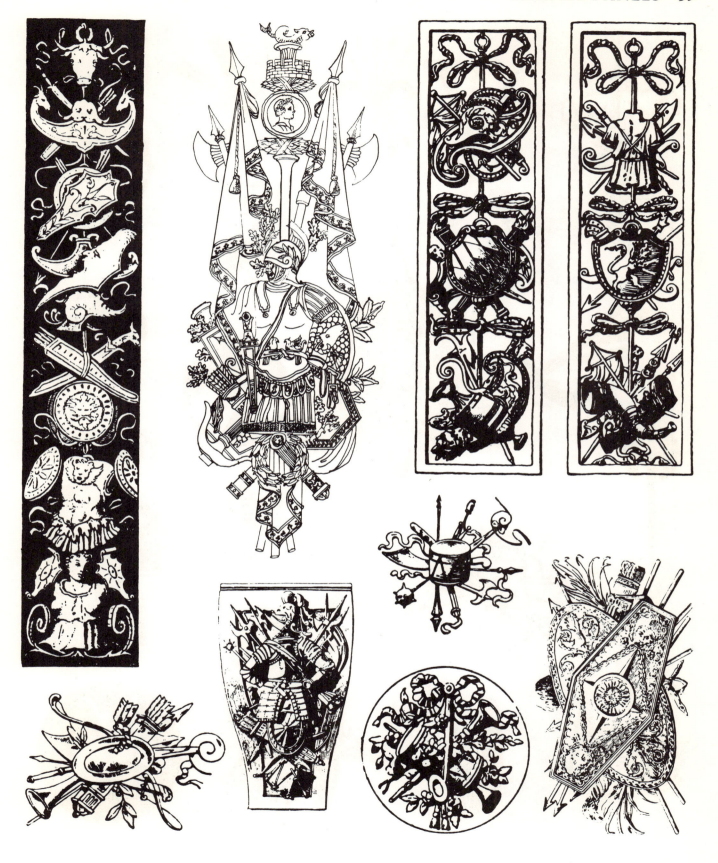

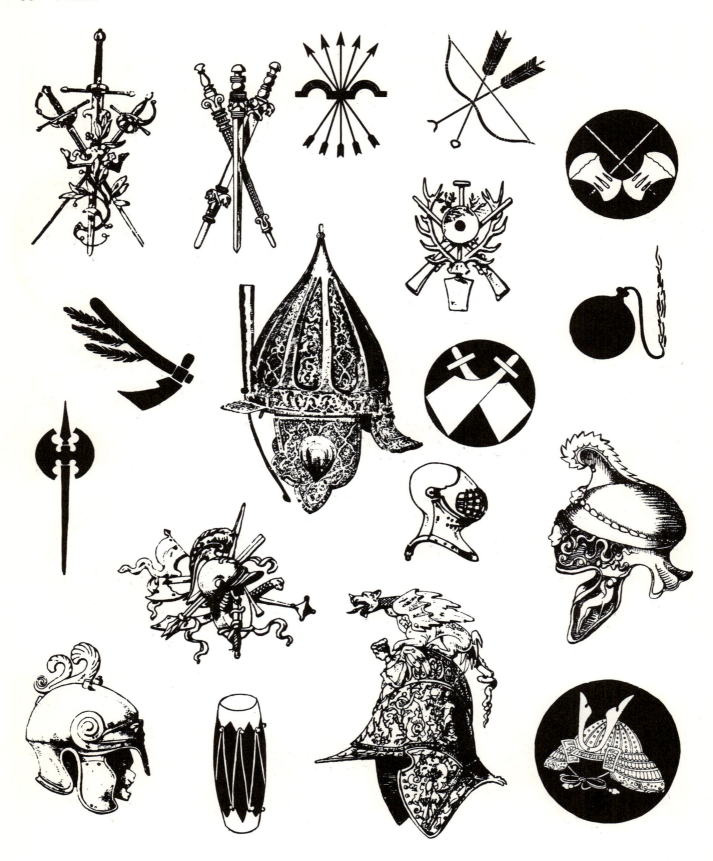

CHAPTER FIVE

Enclosed Space

A N ENCLOSED SPACE in decorative design is defined as an area that is entirely surrounded by a border. Two of the most common examples are rugs and panels. (Borders themselves are literally enclosed spaces, but of a special kind. See Chapter Six.)

An enclosed design is sometimes planned with a vertical center axis and developed to the sides.

Or, the space may be divided into four equal rectangles, with the design starting from the middle of each side and developing toward the center.

The area may also be divided into equal fourths by diagonal lines between the corners, with the decoration starting from the corners.

The space inside the border may contain an all-over pattern (see Chapter Seven), with or without a center motif, or may be broken up by inner squares, diamonds, circles, etc., in any combination.

Naturally, spaces other than rectangles may be enclosed—circles, half-circles, ellipses, diamonds, virtually any shape—although enclosed areas are usually symmetrical or regular.

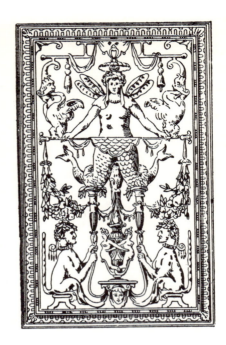

CHAPTER SIX

Bands and Borders

L INEAR PATTERNS known as bands and borders have always been widely used in decorative design, and are found in all periods and styles from the most primitive to the most sophisticated. All borders are bands, but not all bands are borders. A border is the marginal area, usually confined between parallel lines, around the edge of anything. Bands are not limited to an edge, but may also be used as running ornament on a shaft, as a connecting device, as a design for a frieze, or as applied decoration on an architectural element. Bands and borders have a definite width, but no limitation as to length, except as dictated by the total design.

A border begins with a single line and a simple one may consist solely of a series of parallel lines. But if these lines are to result in a well-designed border the thickness of each line and the distances between them must be carefully planned, which requires a thorough knowledge of design principles. Most borders are patterned—that is, constructed of a design repeated at intervals—and moving in only one direction.

Borders are often required to turn corners, which may make the planning complicated. Turning is simplified by using a simple repeat at short intervals, since it allows for more flexibility. In addition to a repeat, a patterned border should appear to have a continuous line running through it, to give it unity. Patterns used in borders should have emphasis and contrast, rhythm, balance, variety and proper value relationships. The border should also be consistently scaled to the design of the area or form it borders.

Just as ornament should be subordinated to the shape, be suitable to the basic design of whatever it

decorates, and *never* compete with it, so a border should frame and enhance the design of the area it surrounds. It is out of place and will destroy the unity of the whole if it attracts too much attention. Lewis F. Day, the highly respected authority on art and design of the late 19th and early 20th centuries, said of a border, "the simpler it is, the better. It is just the simplest borders that are the most difficult to design."

Borders can be classified in many ways, although it is impossible to do so neatly since any system is bound to have design categories that overlap. Also, there would be unavoidable duplication among the illustrations if all kinds of borders were to be clearly shown. One simple classification is as follows:

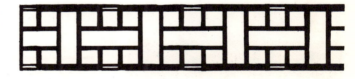

STRAIGHT LINE
1. Simple line—including parallelism
2. Fret and broken fret
3. Zigzag and chevron
4. Variations and combinations

CURVED LINES
1. Wavy
2. Arcs
3. Twists
4. Chain and link
5. Spiral and scroll

COMBINATIONS
1. Chain
2. Counterchange
3. Turnover
4. Interlacing
5. Vertebrate
6. Undulate
7. Broken

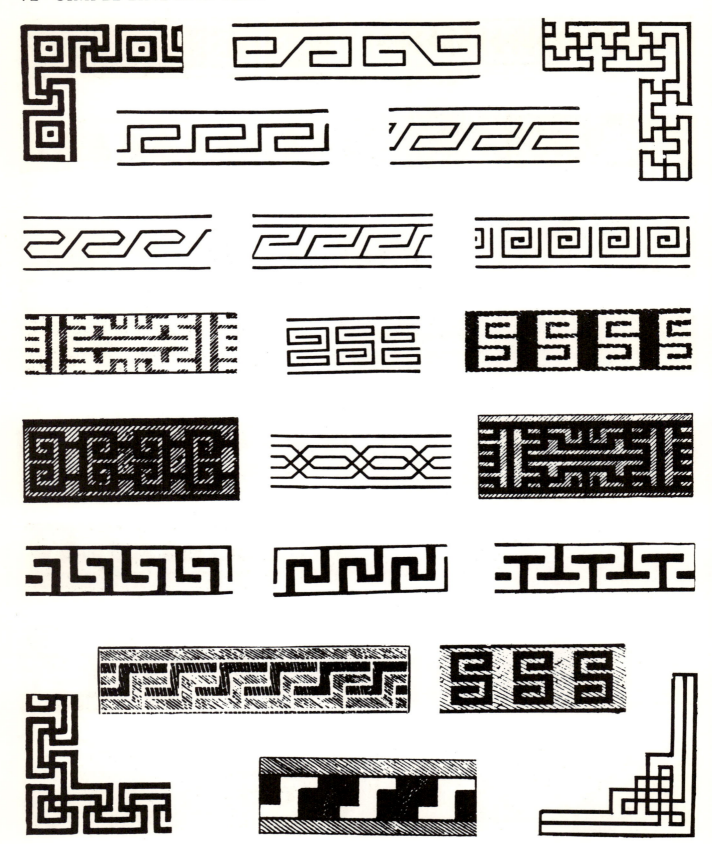

CHAPTER SEVEN

All-over and Repeat Patterns

PATTERN in nature can be seen almost anywhere, wherever there is orderly repetition of form or line. Dandelions or daffodils growing in profusion make a pattern against their green leaves. Pebbles on a path, gravel on a road, the lines on the beach where the surf has been—all make pattern. But man-made pattern, as designed for use on fabrics, wall coverings, floor coverings (both hard and soft surface), or wrapping papers, household linens and many smaller items, is less casual and more regular. It is a system of creating design through the use of similar forms, called repeats, recurring at regular intervals. Surface pattern requires an area to be covered, appropriate and properly decorative motifs, and a system of arrangement suitable for the motifs and the type of design desired. Pattern is two-dimensional, and must be consistent with the shape it is used on.

The design unit or *motif* may be large or small, natural or geometric, traditional or abstract. It can be inspired by almost anything, as long as it is well-designed. Whether it is a simple series of dots, an elaborate Victorian medallion or a sharply angular abstract, it will set the character of the pattern. But the success or failure of the complete design depends

"Sunflowers and Roses," by B. J. Talbert

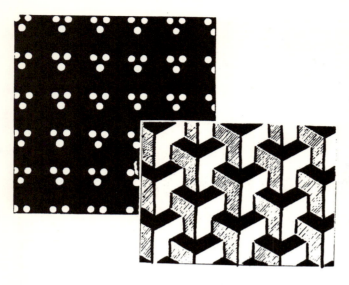

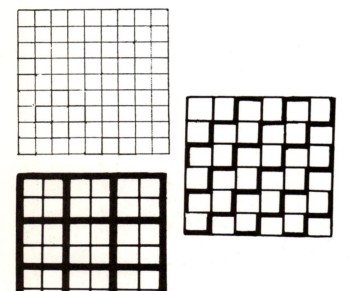

more on the system of arrangement — the rhythm made by the placing of the units on the surface—than on their individual form. Controlled repetition is essential to good pattern. It prevents confusion, assures order and gives scale.

There is a limited number of combinations of lines on which repeated ornament can be arranged. The simplest and most commonly used is a network of crossed lines. On a simple network of square, crossed lines, even without ornament, many different effects can be achieved, either by emphasizing certain lines, or by using color or value on some areas. When ornament is added, the possibilities become endless.

When crossed by diagonal lines, this basic square network is divided into triangles. Two isosceles triangles, with bases together, become a rhombus or diamond; six, with points together, a hexagon. Other networks constructed by emphasizing these forms can be used as a basis for pattern arrangement. An octagon is another figure often used. The illustration below suggests a pattern built on straight lines, and shows how it changes when the basic network remains the same, but the lines are curved. By means of these and similar methods, a great many interesting arrangements can be developed.

A designer starting a repeat design should work out with care the network that will determine the geometric construction on which the pattern will be built. Lines that are visible as a result of the arrange-

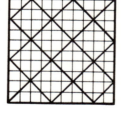 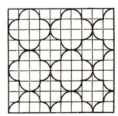

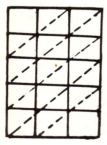 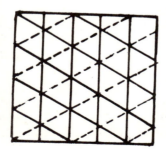  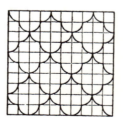 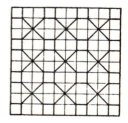

Square *Diamond* *Dropped*

ment of motifs will have an effect on the total design. Pleasing lines are essential to good design. But as repeats increase in number certain details often stand out unintentionally, creating unforseen vertical, horizontal or diagonal stripes, or some unplanned form that interferes with the desired effect. Watch out for such lines or forms that suddenly appear and affect the over-all pattern.

A spiral or scroll, for example, when repeated, can lead the eye in a dizzying rhythm if not properly placed. Accidental stripes can make a wallpaper look crooked on the wall. No matter how well designed an individual motif may be, if it is badly arranged in an all-over pattern the results can be disastrous.

To avoid this, it is necessary to try out the design unit in an area sufficiently large to determine all final effects. By laying out enough motifs it is possible to see the total design, and if the details of the unit create unintended lines that interfere with the over-all design, they can be corrected. Such lines will be sure to affect adversely the rhythm, balance or emphasis of the design and destroy its unity.

Spirals and scrolls must be carefully planned

The spaces between the motifs are also an important part of a design and should never be left to chance, but planned as carefully as the motif itself and its location. It is also necessary to know whether the finished design is to be used flat—for example, on a floor, a chair seat or a table—or vertically, as in curtains, a wall covering, a dress fabric, etc. Also, certain kinds of design that will not do for, say, upholstery fabric that will be stretched flat may be suitable for curtains that will be hung in folds. Both the material to be used and the purpose of the finished product should be carefully considered at an early stage.

Certain systems can be followed in repeating a design unit. One of the most frequently used is called a *drop repeat*. Every other vertical row is "dropped" one-half, two-thirds or a whole unit. As previously emphasized, it is important, when planning, to determine just how the incidental lines will fall. The pattern in this repeat is built on a square, but it also repeats in a diamond. It is a good idea to check the repeat on the basis of both the square and the diamond.

A design based on a square can be turned half way around for an entirely different effect—if it looks well that way. When this is done, the resulting secondary lines will not be the same and must be checked again.

Smaller and simpler repeat patterns, usually made up of spots or sprigs, are built on similar dropped networks. Generally, several such tiny motifs are arranged within one large square which comprises the repeat.

Folding over any kind of motif in a vertical direction makes a symmetrical design sometimes called a *turnover*. Many interesting motifs depend on such a reversal of their lines for good symmetrical design. The reverse repetition is not usually exact, but any changes should be made with care. In some cases, a space is left between the two halves and in others the central strip is not repeated. The turnover can be used with a drop repeat in the same design for still other variations.

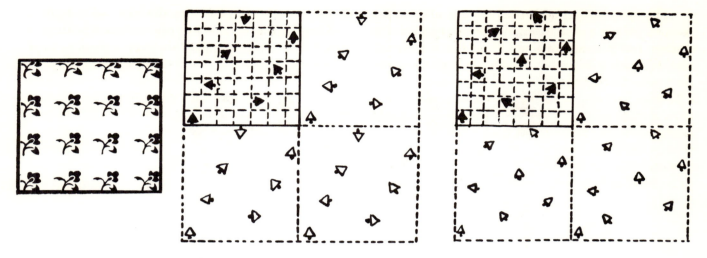

Several tiny motifs are frequently arranged within one larger repeat

Turning over a motif along a central axis assures symmetry

Turnovers

The *turn-around* adds further flexibility to the use of a design motif. A unit may be designed that can be turned around one-half, three-fourths, or completely. Such a unit may extend beyond the square of the complete repeat into the next square, thus avoiding the appearance of a gap in the complete pattern. If the unit is dropped, however, it must be kept within the square.

The term *counterchange,* sometimes *interchange,* is applied to a pattern when a form in a light tone is placed next to the same form in a dark tone. The motif and the ground on which it is repeated alternate in value. The simplest example is a plain check. If a black element is put into the white square and an identical white one into the black square a more complicated counterchange pattern is created. Counterchange is often used in borders as well as in all-over patterns.

Interlacing patterns are particularly well adapted to borders, but are also used in all-over design. Interlacing is the result when lines or bands are inter-woven. It has evolved from early plaiting or braiding and can become very intricate. Beautiful designs can be developed from interlaced lines.

Stripes are often considered to be the simplest of all patterns. But any repeated stripe that has a broken line, or is not perfectly straight, starts a movement in another direction creating an all-over pattern. In fact, most stripes technically are all-over patterns, but when the vertical or horizontal effect is stronger than the all-over, the design is generally identified as a stripe.

Stripes are usually based on one of three kinds of lines—straight, wavy, or chevron. Their success as design will depend on: 1.) the basic character of the motif used, 2.) its spacing, and 3.) the scale and proportion of the width of the bands. Often two motifs, either of which would create a satisfactory stripe pattern, are used together, one superimposed on the other. When this is done, care must be taken to have one dominate; unless it does, the design will be confused and lack unity.

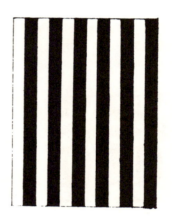
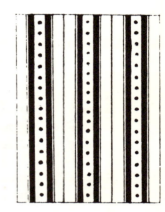

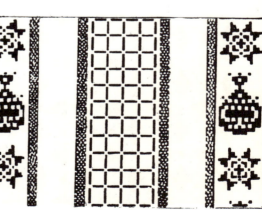

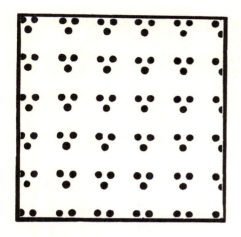

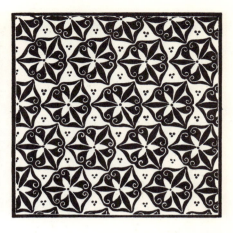

CHAPTER EIGHT

Historic Ornament

STYLES OF DESIGN from entirely different geographical locations and centuries apart in time sometimes have a surprising similarity. This may be because design of an earlier style has influenced a later one. But it is sometimes the result of materials and tools that the two have in common. The character of a style will always be influenced by the materials used and the techniques employed. Throughout history, both factors have affected and occasionally inspired the kind of ornament designed for decoration.

PREHISTORIC, PRIMITIVE AND SAVAGE

The earliest decorative design is classified historically as prehistoric, primitive or savage. Some primitive and savage ornament is also prehistoric. One striking proof that savage design is not always primitive is given in a tattooed human head from New Zealand. The designs in the tattooing are beautifully planned to enhance the shapes and planes of the face and forehead.

Outline was the first method of artistic expression among primitive people. Most early ornament was also linear—at first drawn, later incised on a ground, then colored, and still later carved in flat relief. Generally the forms were geometrical, and geometrical networks were used when forms were repeated. Although not always recognizable, some of the abstract forms represented all or part of the human figure. Natural forms that were used often became stylized, sometimes were completely abstract, and almost always had a magical significance. Frets, rectangular shapes, zigzag or chevron lines, and spirals are the most frequently used elements.

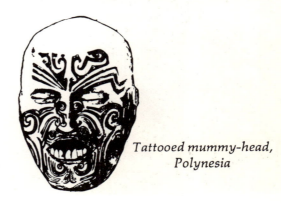

Tattooed mummy-head, Polynesia

PREHISTORIC

Monolithic gate, Tiahuanaco, Mexico

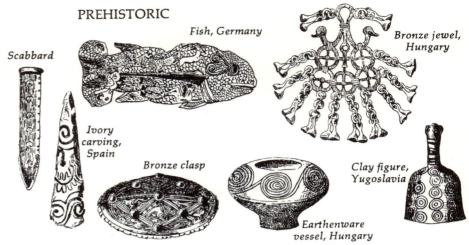

Scabbard

Fish, Germany

Bronze jewel, Hungary

Ivory carving, Spain

Bronze clasp

Clay figure, Yugoslavia

Earthenware vessel, Hungary

PRIMITIVE

Fan screen, Australia

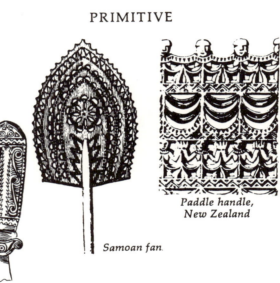

Ebony spatula, New Guinea

Samoan fan

Paddle handle, New Zealand

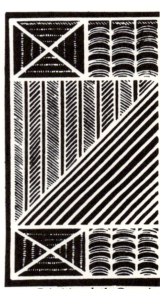

Primitive cloth, Oceania

Ancient Pataka slab

Grass cloth, Samoa

New Zealand club

Whale bone comb, New Zealand

Wovenwork, Australia

EGYPTIAN

Egyptian ornament is unique in the fact that there is no record of its being primitive. Even the earliest examples use both form and color in an effective and appropriate manner. It is known that around 4000 B.C. a kingdom with a highly developed civilization existed in lower Egypt and flourished for thousands of years—the one civilized nation in a world of barbarous ones. Ancient Egyptians led orderly and regular lives—reflected in their design, which is clear, exact and dignified. It is always decorative, simple, refined and unaffected.

Egyptian designers used both natural and geometric forms. The natural forms, while recognizable, were highly stylized. The human figure was usually drawn with the head in profile, the body from the shoulders to the waist in front view, and the lower torso and legs again in profile. Architectural ornament was, on the whole, structural in feeling. Natural forms—appropriately stylized for the purpose—were used in many different ways, with great originality and imagination. Actually, there were few basic motifs, but they were applied with a remarkable amount of variety of treatment.

Color was used freely in Egyptian design, mainly red, yellow and blue and to a less extent green, with black and white for emphasis. Colors were subtle, the reds and yellows going slightly toward brown, blues fairly dark, and greens slightly grayed and yellowed. The colors were all applied perfectly flat, with no shade or shadow. Gradations in tone gave them greater interest and the illusion of depth.

Decorative motifs were developed from plant and animal forms. The most common plant forms were the lotus and the papyrus, and after the XVIII Dynasty the palm. The lotus, considered a symbol of fertility, is illustrated here in different versions. The papyrus, similar in form to the lotus, is equally well suited to varied treatment. The stem of the papyrus, with its base slightly swelling from the root leaves, is often used in the design. The daisy, morning glory, thistle and grape are also found in Egyptian design.

The cobra, frequently found in ornament, was the symbol of death and, because the king had power of life and death, also the symbol of royalty. The vulture, shown with widespread wings, symbolized protection; the wings were also used by themselves with a sun disk. The scarab, symbol of creation and life, represented by a beetle, was a common amulet, and was often found in other jewelry and on mummy cases. The sphinx, a recumbent lion with a human head (if a woman sometimes the bust was also shown) or the head of a ram, symbolized royal or divine power. Feathers of rare birds, carried to kings as emblems of sovereignty, were used in royal insignia. In their adaptation to design they sometimes became scale-like ornament.

Geometric forms included many kinds of zigzags or chevrons, and circles used in different ways, including a variety of rosettes and spiral treatments. Frets were sometimes seen, but mainly as border designs.

The palmette may be based on the lotus. It was not commonly used in Egypt but was passed on to other early design. The anthemion, important in Greek design, developed from the Egyptian palmette.

The three most common column capitals were the bud (single or double), the bell-shaped, and the palmiform. Another, the Hathoric, after the goddess Hathor, was sometimes used.

Bud

Bell

Palmiform

Hathoric

ASSYRIAN

Assyrian design was not particularly original and it is generally thought that the style was largely borrowed from Egypt. Nevertheless it reflects the different social influences, religious beliefs and climatic conditions of the Assyrians. Their ornament was less stiff than the Egyptian and they used more natural forms, with less stylizing. Bulls, lions and other animals, as well as the human figure, were frequently represented.

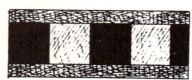

GREEK

In Egypt, color was basic to decorative design, but in Greece, form—through outline, light and shade—supersedes color in importance. The Greeks emphasized pure beauty of line and form, apart from any considerations of religion, symbolism or representation. Their gods and goddesses simply mirrored the life and customs of the people. Their legendary heroes typified physical perfection and their knowledge of the human figure resulted in a standard of natural beauty in sculpture never before known. Their design and ornament had an equal perfection of form. But their basic design was structural, and where ornament was added it was not essential to the appearance of the construction. They used almost no all-over design and developed few patterns.

Greek design and ornament have dignity and grace, vitality and vigor, refinement of proportion, rhythmic movement—all used with artistic restraint. Beautiful stylized adaptations of natural forms indicate a keen observation of nature. Their sculpture reveals a sound knowledge of the human figure and an ability to represent it perfectly in marble.

Some general qualities of Greek ornament are: 1.) simplicity of line, 2.) radiation of parts, 3.) symmetry, 4.) unity, 5.) perfection of detail. Because of these qualities, Greek ornament developed rapidly into design of genuine perfection. The ornament comes from architecture—usually carved, and pottery—usually painted.

The three architectural orders of ancient Greece, used on their columns, were often applied to design and were later adapted by the Romans. The earliest and simplest is the *Doric,* the second, probably the most often used, the *Ionic,* and the third and latest, the *Corinthian,* which adapted the acanthus leaf so skillfully.

The Greeks relied on very few motifs for their ornament, but like the Egyptians applied them in an amazing number and variety of combinations, with genuine originality. The main motifs were:

1. Fret and meander
2. Wave or scroll
3. Spiral, both single and double
4. S curve (called the "line of beauty")
5. Rosette
6. Guilloche
7. Anthemion

Sculpture

Vase painting

Natural foliage forms included the acanthus leaf, an adaptation of the lotus and bud, and the vine—usually laurel, ivy or olive leaves. Animal forms used were versions of the human head, animal heads, including ox skulls, paws, birds and wings. Festoons and swags were made from fruits, flowers and fluttering ribbons, sometimes combined with other motifs.

In architecture, fluting, egg and dart motifs, modillions, dentils, bead and reel patterns, scales and elaborate rinceau versions of the scroll were widely used. Greek architecture, which, like Greek sculpture, reached the highest level of perfection, was known for its beautiful friezes. The columns, like the buildings, were of heroic proportions. The lower part of each column was cleverly designed to swell out slightly (called *entasis*) to compensate for visual distortion which would have made it seem larger at the top.

Doric

Ionic

Corinthian

ROMAN

Etruscan ornament never reached a high state of development, but it was enough ahead of the Romans before Rome conquered Greece to provide what little inspiration the Romans had. The sources of Etruscan ornament have never been determined; but both Asiatic and strong Greek influences are present, suggesting that Etruria was a meeting place of East and West. The Etruscans were especially skilled in bronze and sheet metal work.

Rome was a highly organized military empire in contrast to Greece, which had been a loose confederation of independent states. Her skilled engineers built great buildings, aqueducts and roads, but most of her art was borrowed—although altered to suit the Roman idea. In design, forms similar to the Greek were used, but with more variation and eclecticism, greater elaboration, profusion of detail and exuberance. The refinement, directness and simplicity of Greek design were gone, but Roman ornament was elegant and dramatic. Greek temple design reflected the Greek effort to perfect the arts as a tribute to the gods or to ideal beauty itself. Roman ornament was more concerned with self-glorification.

After conquering Greece in 146 B.C., Rome became mistress of the Western world and began to develop a style of her own, based on Greek prototypes. The Romans adapted and radically modified Greek architectural features—columns, capitals, and horizontal entablature—and developed the semicircular arch. In addition to their versions of the Greek architectural orders, they originated two of their own — *Tuscan* and *Composite*.

The Romans loved luxury and extravagance and their baths and public buildings were particularly elegant, with magnificent coffered ceilings. All ornament was richly carved in high relief. Roman artists were especially fond of continuous spiral lines emanating from a sheaf of acanthus leaves, covered with elaborate foliage and often ending in a rosette. The rinceau is an example of this kind of design. Birds, reptiles, cupids and griffins were often interwined with the foliage. The Greek anthemion was adapted and commonly used. The acanthus leaf appeared in many forms—as a molding ornament, a standing leaf on capitals, a wrapping leaf to mask or provide a base for a branching scroll, or a conventional floral motif to alternate with the anthemion. Roman ornament is alive with acanthus leaves.

The Romans were busy people and their ornament reflects their busyness. Also, their decided preference for magnificence often led to design that was ostentatious and overdone. They were not gifted artistic innovators like the Greeks, and restraint was one thing they never understood.

The Romans invented the pilaster, a flattened portion of a square column, which has been widely used as architectural wall decoration. They were also the first to use the pedestal, which became an important part of both architectural and interior design in the 16th, 17th and 18th centuries. While their columns were not always used structurally, they were used decoratively to good advantage, emphasizing the vertical lines of support.

Laurel

Doric   Ionic   Corinthian   Composite   Tuscan

POMPEIAN

Pompeian design, basically domestic, was in one
sense provincial Roman design, but it suggests other
sources as well. It combined basic Roman motifs with
a lightness of touch that reveals the Greek influence
and was finer and more delicate than Roman design.

Outside of some stucco relief, Pompeian ornament was painted—often the architecture of an entire
room was painted on a flat wall. Usually the dado
and pilasters were black, panels red, and frieze white;
or the dado was black, pilasters red and frieze and
panels white or yellow. Their colors, soft earth pig-
ments, were their own, and were artfully applied to
the exquisite designs that were sketched onto the
panels—their own adaptations of Roman motifs executed with the unmistakable Pompeian feeling.

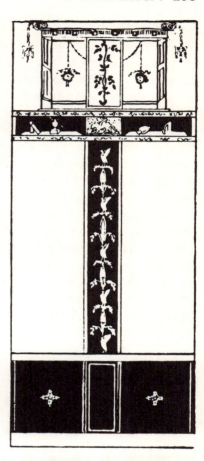

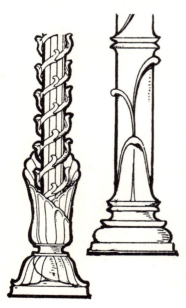

BYZANTINE

The Byzantine style was the result of a coalescence of styles, catalyzed by the increasing importance of Christianity. Under Constantine I, the capital of the Roman Empire was moved to Byzantium, and for the first time Christianity became the official state religion. The style was a mixture of Greek and Roman, Persian and Syrian, plus the Christian influence. It combined the Western knowledge of construction and appreciation of form with the brilliance of Oriental colors.

Sculpture was of secondary importance. Carved decoration was done in low relief, often giving a lacy effect — its light surfaces contrasting sharply with the undercut areas. Surfaces were etched in color, and Byzantium is famous for its beautiful mosaics. The cross and circle, with their Christian symbolism, were frequently used, often interlaced with one another and combined with vines and acanthus.

CELTIC

Although there is some disagreement as to the source of Celtic design, the finest seems to come from Ireland starting in the third century. The Celts are best known for their beautiful manuscripts, metal work and stone carving. They used no foliage or plant forms of any kind in their design. Their patterns are intricate, sometimes geometric, and often based on spiral or interlacing forms. Even birds and animals, as well as snakes, were tremendously elongated and interlaced.

ROMANESQUE

Romanesque design refers to the style of the transitional period between the fall of Rome and the development of Gothic design. Romanesque architecture and ornament is found mainly in churches and monasteries—in Italy, France and Germany, and in England, where it is called Norman. The architecture was characterized by a semicircular arch, known today as the Romanesque arch. The same form was used in ornament. The style was crude in its early phases but developed gradually and reached its peak in France and Germany in the 11th and 12th centuries. Unlike the flat Byzantine surface style, Romanesque art was sculptural, typified by deep cuttings and projections and rich effects of light and shadow. Figure subjects, including animals—particularly the lion and the imaginary griffin—were freely mixed with foliage and conventional ornament.

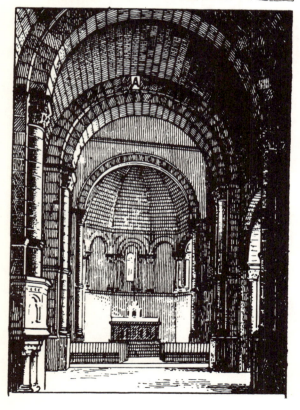

GOTHIC

Gothic design developed from the Romanesque early in the 13th century. Structurally, the styles were similar, but the appearance is very different. The round Romanesque arch was replaced by a pointed arch, giving a new sense of soaring height, windows were greatly enlarged, resulting in a more open and airy feeling, and ornament was much more elaborate.

Gothic design is notable for its beauty of proportion, its variety and the gracefulness and vigor of its ornament. Much of the ornament was structural and the lines of construction are easily seen. Any ornament not related to architectural structure was pictorial or symbolic. Most of the architecture was ecclesiastical.

Gothic design started in France and, with the exception of England, which developed an independent Gothic style, other countries borrowed from France both general design and details. Italy used some Gothic design in buildings, but never developed a true Gothic style.

The acanthus leaf gradually disappeared; the artists and craftsmen who did the carving turned to ordinary vegetation for inspiration and began to develop a new foliage. At first it was stiff, but slowly it evolved into beautiful design, suitable for architecture, with unusually graceful, delicate detail. Human figures were used and they also had a strong architectural quality, often elongated, with clothing in stylized, vertical folds.

MOHAMMEDAN

Mohammedan art can be roughly divided into several types, which differ only in superficial ways. Those most often seen in our design are Persian, Arabic and Moorish, the latter as interpreted by the Moors in Spain.

The *Persians* were conquered by the Mohammedans in 632. Persian art was essentially decorative and combined a beauty of form with pure color. Plant and flower forms were used, such as the tulip, rose, hyacinth, iris and pine and were natural, not stylized. Persian designs influenced the design of European textiles in the 16th and 17th centuries.

Very early in their history, the *Arabs* created and perfected their own style of art and design, based on traditional Persian art, but developing differently. Their design combined simple general forms with decoration that was refined and elegant. The Koran prohibited the use of representational art so there are almost no human figures or animals. Arabesques based on floral motifs are so conventionalized that they lose their resemblance to flowers. Inscriptions taken from texts of the Koran were often interwoven into the design. Arabian ornament is made up of flowing, interlacing and symmetrical lines, arranged geometrically.

Moorish design and art, as developed in Spain, is typified by the Alhambra. The style is similar to the Arabian, but is more complex, distributes the design better and uses more flowing foliage and arabesques. Decorative ornament is always subordinate and conforms to the basic structure of the whole. The lines, with intricate arabesques, angular geometric pattern and Arabic calligraphy, are perfectly combined to create a beautiful unified effect. Although elaborate, they are not overdone. The Moors made dramatic use of color, relying mainly on primary colors—blue, red and gold—and using the secondary colors—purple, green and orange—for less important areas, such as dadoes.

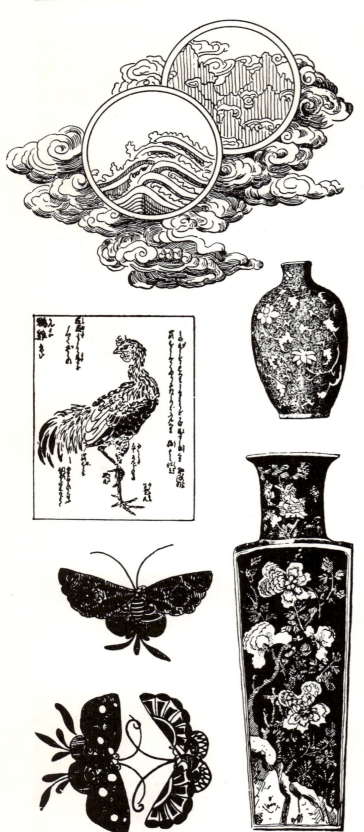

CHINESE

Although Chinese art goes back to mythical times of great antiquity, it has not changed radically over the centuries. Architecturally, the Chinese have adhered closely to one type of design, and are probably best known for their pagodas and the peaked roof with upturned, overhanging eaves. However, while some beautiful buildings exist—notably the Imperial Palace at Peking—Chinese architecture rarely attained the heights of perfection frequently reached by Chinese painting, sculpture and pottery.

China's decorative arts were luxuriant, and included textiles, wood and jade carvings, bronzes, enamels and resplendent embroideries. Ornament was rich in symbolism based on myths and traditions. Many natural subjects were used—peonies, chrysanthemums, bamboo, numerous other plants and flowers, stylized waves and clouds, butterflies, birds, animals and such imaginary creatures as dragons and phoenixes. Geometric forms, including a great variety of frets, were also widely utilized.

European art and design was influenced by the Chinese after trade with the Far East began. At one time Chinese design became very popular in the West and was adapted, often beautifully, particularly in France—where it was called *chinoiserie.*

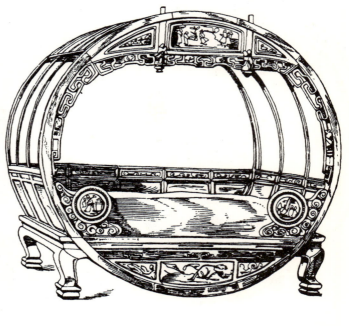

JAPANESE

Japanese art and design had its origin in China, but soon developed an individuality of its own that had much more variety than Chinese art. Similar motifs were used—flowers, birds such as the peacock, pheasant and crane as well as many smaller ones, fish, insects, animals and reptiles. Cherry, plum and pine trees, fruit blossoms, and natural phenomena such as snow-clad mountains often appear. The fan was considered a symbol of life, and many different kinds are found in design. The Japanese also made beautiful swords and often the designs of the weapons or details from their mounts are used in ornament.

Japanese designs and motifs combine a keenly observed and literal interpretation of an object with an exceptionally clever and ingenious kind of conventionalizing. A great many natural forms are used, highly stylized in their adaptation. The Japanese are able to vary a single design in many ways and fit most of their motifs into arbitrary shapes or borders.

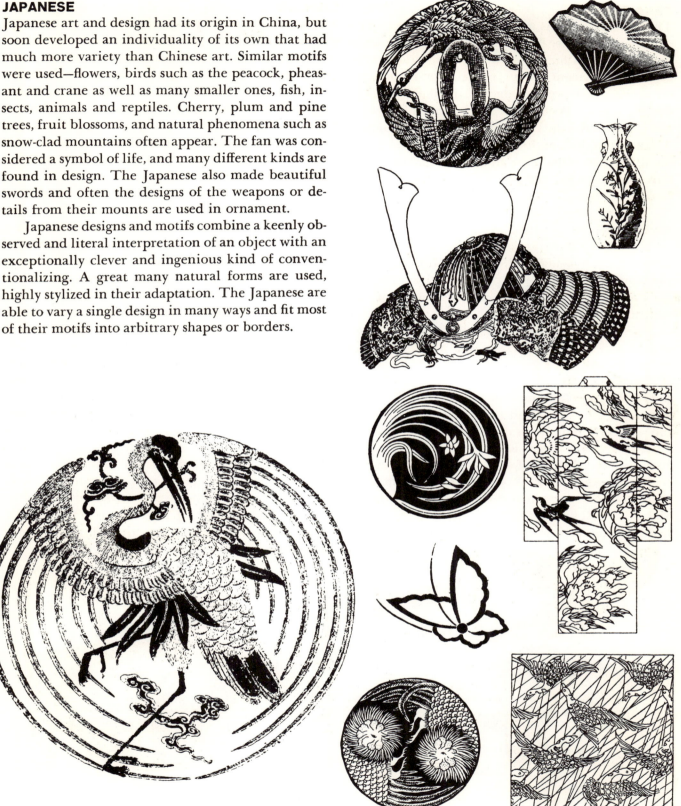

RENAISSANCE

The Renaissance was marked by a developing spirit of inquiry and an end to the complete domination of the arts by the Church. Beauty of proportion, unity of parts, refinement of line and detail and symmetrical arrangement were characteristic of Renaissance design, which was classic in inspiration. Much of it was based on Roman design, but it was never copied. The acanthus leaf, anthemion, rinceau, egg and dart, modillion and dental were all freely used, but the details were changed and new and original combinations devised.

The first part of the Renaissance was transitional, marking the change from Gothic to classicism.

During the second period—1500-1600—the art of design reached its highest level. The Church was still the main patron of the arts, but wealthy princes in Italy and kings and noblemen in France provided additional patronage.

The third period, called *Baroque,* was characterized by a revolt against classicism. Much design of the period was gaudy and overdone, but by no means all. Ornament was large in scale, restless and opulent, and full of curves and movement, with much applied stucco and gilt. But it had its own definite character and some of it is dramatically beautiful.

The *Rococo* design in Italy was similar to the Baroque, and developed from it toward the end of the earlier period. The Rococo was smaller in scale, with more delicate ornament, using wreaths, shells, arabesques, all kinds of ribbons, and foliage, flowers, fruit, festoons and swags.

In France, the *Louis XIV* period was contemporary with the Baroque and the design was similar in scale and ornament, but structurally more restrained and classic. Both styles were elegant and magnificent.

The *Louis XV* style was contemporary with the Rococo, but the design and ornament were finer.

The design of the *Louis XVI* period in France saw a return to the classic. The excavations at Pompei gave designers new classic inspiration. Motifs included rosettes, festoons and swags, urns, pine cones and architectural fluting, frets and beads. Flowers and leaves were used with ribbons and baskets. Architecture made use of trophy panels, either carved or painted on the wall within the panel molding.

The *Directoire* period immediately following continued the classic trend, showing an even stronger Pompeian influence. Motifs, in addition to the classic ones, were military—trumpets, drums, stars, spears, etc.

The *Adam brothers* in England were contemporary with this classic period in France. Their interiors and furniture were decorated with a variety of classic ornament, including such motifs as animal heads, scrolls, festoons, urns, drapery swags, lyres, fluting and medallions.

French *Empire* design was strongly classic, influenced by Greek, Roman and Egyptian forms. It was not classic at its best, and much of it was pompous, formal and heavy. Many different kinds of ornament were used in the decoration of architecture and furniture. Military motifs were prominent, and Napoleon brought back from Egypt such exotic devices as obelisks, winged sphinxes and lions, swans and cobras. Many old familiar classic motifs were also used.

ART NOUVEAU

A design trend which did not develop into a genuine style, *Art Nouveau* started in Belgium in the 1890's and became popular in France around the turn of the century. It was basically a protest against aping traditional design. Just as Louis XV designers had reacted to the classicism of the preceding period by totally ignoring it and building their design on free-hand curves used asymmetrically—so did Art Nouveau designers. The design motifs were naturalistic, with long, flowing curved lines that had little relationship to structure. Art Nouveau, though by no means consistently good, was responsible for introducing entirely new decorative effects, some of which were beautiful.

MODERN

The term *Modern,* as used in connection with ornament and design, refers to many different kinds of design and often becomes confusing. No typical examples, such as those that illustrate the periods of the past, exist. Since the time of the Art Nouveau a succession of trends have come and gone. Some have been better and less fleeting than others and have contributed to design in general. The German Bauhaus group and the "less is more" philosophy of Mies Van der Rohe had a profound influence on architectural design, but made little use of ornament. There are no stock motifs for modern design, such as the Egyptian lotus, the Greek anthemion, or the Renaissance arabesque. But many beautiful designs are being created today, some of which may eventually be considered typical of today's design. A few examples of good contemporary ornamental design and pattern are shown.

*"Eden." A Win Anderson Fabrics Design
by the Larsen Design Studio*

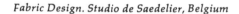

Fabric Design. Studio de Saedelier, Belgium

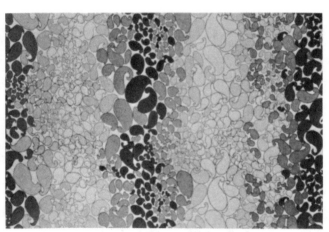

*"Thousand Islands." A Win Anderson Fabrics Design
by the Larsen Design Studio*

"Print Nouveau." A Jack Lenor Larsen, Inc. Design

(Not to be reproduced without permission.)

Hungarian

Greek

Spanish

Pennsylvania Dutch

Finnish

Hungarian

Polish

Russian

Danish

Yugoslavian

Pennsylvania
Dutch

Finnish

Russian

Norwegian